Afte

thoughts from a GRUMPY innovator

written & illustrated by costas papaikonomou

This is the first edition, September 2020

Twitter: @grumpyinnovator
Email: costas@grumpyinnovator.com
Web: grumpyinnovator.com

ISBN 979-868-286-3112

to Patricia, Spiro and Dimi
thank you for your patience with me in
the past looong twelve years

[**In the end, we're all just a persona in someone's segmentation study.**]

After-Thoughts

In 2012, I published the first Grumpy Innovator book about the ugly reality of innovation in corporate environments. Then in 2015, I assembled a follow-up to outline why not all innovation is equal. In both cases, the responses have been heart-warming. Strangers invited me to present on stage. I found like-minded individuals operating in very different industries. It put me in touch with people navigating business risk in different ways.

Readers have been ever so nice.

- "When's the serious book coming where you share the exciting confidential stuff? I want to know how others mess up."
- "Please use more absorbent paper next time. I'm into cradle to cradle use of paper."
- "Did you draw these cartoons yourself? They're funny! But keep your day job."
- "Can you write something about small orgs too? Surely, they're struggling as much as us big businesses. It's unfair you pick on us."

Now in 2020, I thought it might be a good time to collate a third book and call it a trilogy. The first came out after we had gained traction with our innovation agency Happen Group. The second when we had become established player in the innovation world. Now we have sold the business and become part of a truly global organisation. A new stage, next life, new insights. A moment to take stock.

Also, the world has changed a little since 2015. Generation-Z is now well established, people bore us with memes and Fake News every day, and the next mega crisis has hit us in the form of a virus that is destructive biologically, financially and politically.

Regardless of all this (or because of) you'll be happy to know that I'm still quite grumpy. But less than previously, and perhaps because I'm older I feel an urge to reveal what actually works in this space. Imagine something between a TED talk, a coming out on Oprah, and outright lecturing.

I've compiled the following for you;

Premise: Why Innovation Isn't As Sexy As Business Books Promise

As a rule of thumb, there are only two routes in innovation. One is about sleepless nights, pain & hardship. The other is about sleepless nights, pain and hardship, plus divorce & financial ruin. This is not what the business books are promising.

Unfairly, the word 'innovation' is mostly used to describe with hindsight what someone has already done, and done successfully enough to get noticed. Winner's bias. Attention is skewed to the few entrepreneurs who hit the jackpot, not to the many thousands of people in regular businesses who create new products and services every day. Nor the countless failed entrepreneurs whose ideas brought them nothing but debt and ulcers.

The fancy chatter about disruption by start-ups with nothing to lose isn't much help either, when you're still at the front end of the journey wondering what to do next – with *everything* to lose. Besides, the chances of the world needing yet another digital platform Ponzi scheme that might succeed isn't very high. In all likelihood, you need to create something new *within* the tightly confined space of your employer's business model and market.

Should you then copy the habits of the successful businesspeople who smile at us from magazine covers and LinkedIn posts? Well, unsuccessful innovators show many of the same stubborn behaviours, so that probably won't work either.

Creativity gurus will claim you need to get out of your comfort zone in order to achieve new things successfully. The further the better – blatantly ignoring that most people tasked with creating the next big thing already are deeply uncomfortable with that assignment. If anything, *more* comfort is what you need for good ideas, not less. Long car rides and hot showers to let your mind wander, rather than your boss's ambitious KPI's to stress over.

A simple yet mostly overlooked first step up and out of that place of discomfort is to move attention away from what the idea will *be*, to what it needs to *deliver*. Almost all innovation initiatives are commercially driven by someone wanting to make money with their new idea. From start-ups to corporate giants, that new idea's sole purpose is to displace something else. Whether it's a small change to annoy a direct competitor, or a big one to overturn a whole industry, it starts with acknowledging what that new idea must *do* in order to be considered a success. Without that acknowledgement, it's simply impossible to adequately judge how radical an idea needs to be to make the impact you want.

Counter to typical business book arguments, you then want to find the *least* radical solution possible, because the less disruptive it is, the easier it will be to implement. A big reason so many innovations fail is not because the market won't accept them, but that they're too disruptive for the business itself to implement and sustain profitably. If the market wants a new flavour, don't bet the ranch by developing a whole new product with all the problems that come with it. And if you spot a very big unmet need that might overturn the whole industry, then you *still* need to find the simplest of solutions to answer it, ideally with a product or service very similar to what you're already making. The size of the unmet need being resolved is what counts. Not the disruptiveness of the solution.

If you're wondering what that means in practice, here's one example – and the only product example I will share – from our history at Happen Group. Working with a cough syrups manufacturer, their ambition was no less than completely revolutionizing that market. A very mature market, with established rules and dominant competitors. We knew we needed to find a *massive* unmet need in order to make such an impact, and the stakes were clearly against us. But we realized quickly a weak spot in most of the market research floating around for the 'cough & cold' category. It was all based on quant surveys and focus groups amongst people who were perfectly healthy and asked to *remember* what it was like to have a cough. No wonder no one ever spotted something new to do.

Instead, we quickly drummed up a few friends and family members who were *actually ill* and convinced them it would be a good idea for a few of our team members to come spend time with them. We tailed them for a couple of days and found heaps of unmet needs. Small ones, like the nuisance of knowing the sore throat is coming but not *when*. Or figuring out what kind of cough a sick child has. And we found the big one too. Or actually, a small one but true for nearly everyone: without exception, every sick individual struggled at the pharmacy or drugstore, when they needed to pick the right type of cough medicine. Was it a chesty cough, a tickly cough or a dry cough? We saw some cough in the face of the pharmacist, desperately asking "what kind of cough do you think it is?".

Bingo. Big need identified. Now all we had to do was *not* come up with a fancy solution. Not an app to cough in for medical advice, not a shelf navigation system. Our client made cough syrups for OTC retail, we needed a solution that would fit them and disrupt the market, not disrupt their own business model. A solution that would fully satisfy that unmet need of not knowing what kind of cough you have, easy to manufacture for our client and hard to follow for competition. So we created a cough syrup *for all coughs.* It went straight to #2 in the launch market in its first cough season.

Based on many years at Happen Group, helping teams innovate successfully in very mature and crowded markets, there seem to be four distinct areas that dramatically affect success rates along the innovation journey.

- **Clarity on the business objective**
- **Uncover insight you can act upon**
- **Create commercially viable ideas**
- **Energize the business into action**

Successful innovation in popular business media looks sexy and aspirational. You'll see in that list above that the ugly reality is that it isn't really that ugly, just a little less magical. More than anything, it's a skill you can learn and become good at, both on a personal and a business-level.

There's no magic ingredient here, just lots of good cooking. Let's dive in.

Costas Papaikonomou
August 2020

Business objective aligned	Consumer insights you can act upon	Commercially viable ideas	Team energy & commitment	=	**INNOVATION SUCCESS**
X	Consumer insights you can act upon	Commercially viable ideas	Team energy & commitment	=	WRONG PRODUCTS
Business objective aligned	X	Commercially viable ideas	Team energy & commitment	=	PRODUCTS THAT NO ONE WANTS
Business objective aligned	Consumer insights you can act upon	X	Team energy & commitment	=	PRODUCTS THAT BANKRUPT YOU
Business objective aligned	Consumer insights you can act upon	Commercially viable ideas	X	=	ENDLESS FRUSTRATION

Never Change For Change's Sake

I KNOW OUR CONSUMERS LOVE THE OLD MODEL, BUT IF I DON'T CHANGE IT HOW WILL ANYONE KNOW I'M IN CHARGE?

Never Change For Change's Sake

Great innovation comes from clarity of what the business objective is, which the innovation is required to deliver in market. This is universally misunderstood. All too often an innovation project within large corporate entities start with defining the type of idea that is necessary, for example "We need the next [widget], with refills like Nespresso®".

Consider innovation a spectrum of activities, with a range of different outcomes: are you innovating to protect, grow or transform your business? By chunking it down to these three impact levels, each with its own definitions of success, restrictions and approaches to get there, clarity of thought comes much easier. For instance, one shouldn't try to create a revolutionary and expensive new product design if the business objective is merely to steal a little share. Equally, if the time has come to transform the business, one shouldn't be restricted by current technical (i.e. manufacturing) capabilities.

It might be that the over-emphasis of disruptive innovation in the past decade, combined with winner's bias, has made game changers all too much the benchmark for what good innovation looks like. The reality is different – managing innovation is less about spawning radical ideas and more about rigorous portfolio management. Businesses who maintain their portfolio durably over decades all judge well when it's time to create a new platform and when milking the old one will do.

The overarching principle that has garnered some consensus with is that ~70% of resources should be targeted on 'core renovation', ~20% in 'innovation for growth' and the remaining ~10% on transformational innovation.

Second
thoughts from a
GRUMPY
innovator

So, how to set that balance? It's a fairly top-down conversation that needs to happen, tightly connected to the overall business/growth strategy. I'll skip going into the weeds of how this can play out across different brands, and call out the types of questions on should answer and agree upon;

- Clarify the business challenge to address for the brand in question. This is about being specific about what the portfolio needs to achieve in market, with your customers and consumers. This is externally focused. Not some hair-splitting debate on brand purpose.
- Agree the type of innovation required for which parts of your brand's portfolio; protect, grow or transform? Or NO innovation, which is an overlooked, very legitimate choice if things are in good shape and growing already.
- Be crystal clear about the target consumer and changing relationship with them that you're after.
- Review emerging signals of change that can be leveraged too drive your brand's agenda more easily. There's no harm in piggybacking on a theme that's front-of-mind for the people you are trying to please.
- Recognize the obstacles to success; R&D, people, channel, factory, politics, budget, culture. Call them out and adapt either the resource, or your plans accordingly.

"Yes mr Bond, this nuclear fusion technology could power the world 100% green, and before your eyes I will now PATENT it." – Blofeld's corporate brother

If you run a 1-person operation and insist on labeling yourself 'President and CEO' on LinkedIn, please also add accountant, typist, mail room manager and cleaner.

You lost me at 'EPIC'.

'Follow your Dreams!'
– *winner's bias.*

"It's easier to commoditize something premium, than to premiumize a commodity"
* Contemplates brilliance of that aphorism while sipping a $6 cappuccino *

REAL INNOVATION HEROES
First person to dice onions for the second time
First person to wonder what aspartame tastes like
First person to consider an indoor toilet
First person to assume that wolf could be tamed

Do whatever you fear competition would do.

If you were looking to start a business in the transport sector, for about 8000 years your best bet would have been something with horses.

Just like the Hydra kept growing new heads, is there an analogy for something that keeps growing new feet to shoot?

In a shrinking market, the last thing you want to do is copy your competition. Instead: look for the gaps, the other categories your business has leaked away to, the unmet needs you've been missing all along.

Truly disruptive innovation looks like magic, at first.

Gentle reminder that at the time of writing of this book, the oldest Millennials are pushing 40 and have in fact become quite square - and fat.

Gandhi: "It is the quality of our work which will please God and not the quantity."
Data Aggregator: "Uhm yes, Mahatma can we talk for a sec please thanks.""

For a computer aimed at 'Creatives', why do most MacBook users keep the standard snow-capped mountain as desktop? Meh.

Every time you say Millennial, a Baby Boomer dies.

[

HEART (insight, why)
GUT (intuition, what)
BRAIN (technology, how)
Progress drivers are old as human nature.
Older than TED talks even.

]

Where GenX spends their lives looking for cheap versions of luxury shit, Millennials spend their time looking for luxury versions of cheap shit. Meanwhile Boomers had the luxury shit, and GenZ can't be bothered.

Paradoxically, it seems quite disruptive nowadays not to have a disruptive innovation strategy.

The real leader eats last.
The real frequent flyer boards last too.

Thought from a friend on how to act in life:
"Behave like you are an ancestor. Because you are one, of many generations to come."
Puts things like binge-watching Netflix as a hobby into an interesting perspective.

Recycling wasn't "invented" at some point. It was the normal way of life since the dawn of humankind, and still is, for everyone except for city dwellers in the past ~100 years. Who promptly elevated it to a virtue signal.

You can recognize the hardcore Zoom/Teams user by their casual muting/unmuting to insert a nonchalant 'hmmm'.

Niche, Nitch or Neesh? Asking for a friend.

Organisational change MUST involve product innovation. Why else modernize organisations around the crappy products that got them in trouble?

A tell-tale sign of a category still in its embryonic stage is the number of quacks and frauds still operating at a profit.

Forget about creating disruptive product formats if your procurement team needs 12 months to register and approve new suppliers.

Commodities don't go extinct but evolve into posh virtue signallers. Horse-riding, gasoline old-timers, scratch cooking, vinyl audio, meat-free diets, paper books and now even vaccines.

Whenever I hear a 20-something start-up CEO talk about 'fulfilling a life-long dream' I'm reminded I have socks older than that dream.

Places NOT to be rushed & hurried:
Operating theatre; Cactus farm; Domino toppling competition; Paris CDG

For anti-fragile innovation, ask yourself:
- Am I placing multiple small, low risk bets?
- Would a perfect outcome on one of my little bets reap something huge, or merely something small?

'Instead of WHAT will people use this?'
#ForgottenInnovationQuestions

If you always expect to fail, then you'll certainly celebrate being right a lot of the time.

'Age of Disruption' anagrams 'Aspired Goof Unit'

Divorce lawyers applaud countries that legalize same-sex marriage. Just imagine: 10% market growth overnight!

Wow. In a little chat with my local bakery owner, we realised he made $2.8 Bn more profit than Uber last year. He must be a good baker.

If words are not enough to convey the depth of your message, use Kung Fu.

Winner's bias. It's only human. Literally, down to every single one of (y)our genes.

IT Security Paradox: The more often I am asked to update my password, the simpler the password I create.

Given that eventually someone will disrupt your business anyway, you might as well disrupt it yourself, no?

** Innovation Conundrum **
Increased focus on breakthrough: good.
Neglect your core: not good.

Are ya'all still 3D printing?

'Turn lucky strikes into winning streaks' – the essence of good business.

Kickstarter idea: a Kickstarter function that checks if the applicant's idea already exists in better form elsewhere, and then orders it straight from Alibaba.

WHY IT TAKES FOREVER TO FIND THE BIG IDEA

If you could go back to 2005, what would you invest in? Tattoo ink; Gorilla glass; Marvel comics; Kale.

From a risk management pov, there's no difference between carrying all your eggs in one basket or hauling one massive ostrich egg.

Fanatics adapt their behaviour to achieve a goal. The mainstream doesn't. Now think again about what your sustainability initiatives are asking of your audience.

Accidentally typed 'Wealth & Hellbeing' and now I think I'm on to something.

Beware of the competitor with
1) Deep pockets
2) Long term agenda
Because
1) = You haemorrhage fast
2) = You die slowly
1)+2) = Better quit and join them

When putting hypotheses out to field, please take care these are statements you could agree or disagree with. "I care about the environment" or "recycling is important" are not going to evoke a lot of debate. Include the trade-off in your statement.

['Fail Fast' isn't an excuse to 'Fail Often']

The innovation team's job is to make their business anti-fragile to the inevitable change in the market.

Most incubators are in fact outcubators.

Asking for a 2nd opinion because you don't like the 1st one doesn't mean you'll get a better one.

Don't talk about the strength of your brand if smaller start-ups are hammering you in the marketplace.

What doesn't help is that top-down intervention tends to be driven by belief that everything is top-down organised to start with.

[**The most realistic predictions on A.I. in the original Terminator® movie were:**
- Looking up a name in the phone book.
- Recognizing a face.
- Deepfaking voices.
- Driving a car, wildly.
- Shooting the wrong person.]

'Losing is the new Winning' – a dear (but anonymous) innovation friend of mine.

Moving confidently with little information: how experts and idiots operate in similar ways.

[**It strikes me how innovation teams everywhere seem to be looking for new ways of working. This is good. What is less good is the lack of interest in proven results of these new ways of working.**]

'Hominem unius libri timeo' 'I fear the man of a single book' – Saint Thomas Aquinas on fanatic readers of popular business books.

There are so many leaders courses on offer in my LinkedIn feed that I'm starting to wonder if there are any minions left to do the actual work.

Hey HR manager, before sending the team out on an Organic Mindfulness Rebirthing course, how about some basic PowerPoint training, hmm?

Sometimes it's good to pause to not think.

A brand innovation objective of creating "behaviour change" sounds to me more befitting a kindergarten or penitentiary, no?

I SAID *BE CURIOUS* LIKE A CHILD.
NOT *ACT* LIKE A CHILD.

What Facebook shows to business, is that the only way to win at the casino is to own the casino.

Hey Entrepreneur, *NEVER EVER* take advice on running your business from an academic. And that includes their books. Because: they're academics.

Want things to happen at the right moment? Initiate them yourself.

The difference between mere 'new' and actual 'progress' is that with the latter, you cannot go back.

Headaches are not caused by lack of Aspirin.

Hey Entrepreneur, remember: if you're burning someone else's cash instead of your own, you're technically not an entrepreneur.

Is it the start-up's idea that is disrupting the market, or the tsunami if capital behind it?

The difference between 'Game Changer' and 'core renovation' is 'Vision and Willpower' versus 'objectives and a budget'.

Opportunities & implications of platform design? Next time you see a Bentley, yell: "Hey, nice Volkswagen!" and you'll learn the difference.

I wonder if AirBnB®'s original startup VC pitch was: "We're like Tinder®, but family-friendly".

I suspect fancier tools lead to fancier dreams, not fancier outputs.

If you put your 3Y growth plans next to those of your competitors, the combined category would be 200% in that period. At least one of you is lying.

Heading home after a nice week in the US, a country where everything is doubled, tripled and quadrupled, except the layers of toilet paper.

Aha! We meet again, LHR-T4 G23... You devious little massive detour.

Game Changers destroy, before they create.

I've analysed this 2nd Tech Bubble and found the main difference with the 1st one is that back then, we all thought Hammer pants were cool.

Pray your competitors also have no time for vision or strategy.

Clichés. Annoying, but true.

A: "We should launch a game changer, now."
B: "Then build a time machine."
A: "Why, to steal an idea from the future?"
B: "No, to launch 30 years ago."

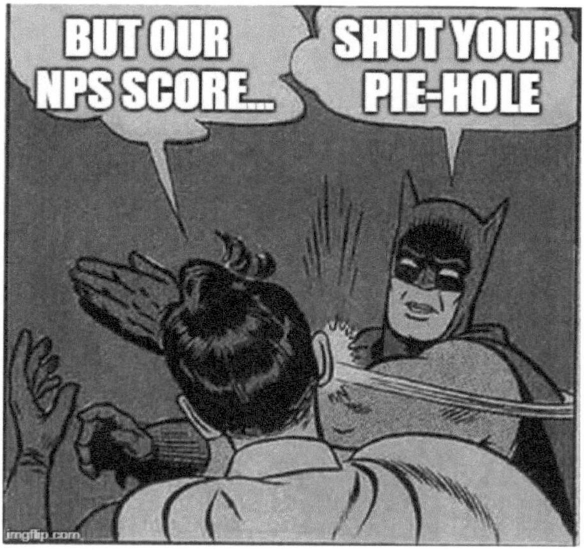

Nothing beats arguing with people who know what they're talking about. Because even if you lose, you win... new insight.

Is your 3Y strategy assuming a static competitive field, or a dynamic one full of people even more eager than you are?

"Build it and they will come" – what every innovator thinks deep down, even those with an acquisition & retention strategy.

[**Hey Manager, by far the easiest way to connect to the different pillars in the business is to rotate where in the canteen you sit for lunch.**]

Before taking any think-tank's New Year's predictions too seriously, read up on their previous New Year predictions.

The reason 95% of innovation fails might well be that in 95% of cases, a much smaller change would have been enough & far easier to achieve.

"What do you mean, there isn't a shortcut?!" – Generation Z growing up into adults.

Start-ups seem to be naming their businesses like IKEA names its furniture.

The only difference between "we want to be #1" and "WE WANT TO BE 3!" is pressing the shift key on a UK QWERTY keyboard.

Breaking news on "Well-being" need-state! It turns out to be "Vanity" in disguise.

Asking for disruptive innovation? Be aware you're asking to disrupt your business first.

Don't plan for change only. Plan for the new normal.

It takes a different kind of sales pitch to get people to spend their own money. Because spending someone else's money is easy.

It's quite depressing how "start-up" has become synonymous with "no viable business model" and that this isn't considered to be much of a problem.

Make the act of delivering game-changing innovation more palatable by first listing all the things you can keep the same. Quite a lot, usually.

It's national "Innovation Day" today. For statistical accuracy, every other day this year is "Failed Innovation Day".

Hey crisis manager: what have you undone for me lately?

"Welcome to the future! And again! I mean now, the future! Stay with me, future's here!" – Futurologist trying to get his timing just right.

Hey start-up, for the umpteenth time: the most important thing isn't cash, but cashFLOW. Make some money instead of just burning it.

[**Many innovations fail, not because the market won't accept them, but they're too disruptive for the business itself to sustain profitably.**]

Remember that your consumers' understanding of your category is about as precise as your own knowledge of say, the nuances of motor oil selection.

A mechanical design teacher once explained to me that 1 micron is what you smell on your finger after wiping with 1-ply. Wise man.

The only truly non-renewable resource is TIME.

"But we always do it this way!" – Organisational change team being asked to stop changing organisations for change's sake.

Hey Marketer, you cannot blame the audience for messing up your magic trick.

If you are the category leader, you should be the one setting the trends. Don't go searching through decks for trends to follow.

**[Bootstrapping.
The wantrepreneur's worst fear looking out. The entrepreneur's proudest achievement looking back.]**

For people using your services all the time, "Less User Experience" will be welcomed as "Better User Experience". Get out of their face.

Need an idiot-proof concept? Go talk to idiots for inspiration.

Don't bother revolutionising your own category. Too difficult and expensive. Revolutionise someone else's. Much easier and cheaper.

No matter what excuse you have, giving stuff away for free is not a business model. Because 'no business'.

Oil tanker metaphors often miss a part. Yes, they are slow to turn around. But once they move in the right direction, they're unstoppable.

Have you noticed how successful digital platforms are in fact examples of a back-office becoming the front-office?

If 'fighting boredom' is the angel investor's main driver, beware of excessive interference. All outside investors have an agenda.

"Ambition, Concept, Develop, Engineer, Hone, Implement, Launch, Nurture, Success, Win" – the sequence you'll only find in the dictionary.

Comfort yourself with the idea that competition is probably spending just as much time carefully planning.

Simplification is about letting go, not about summarising.

Turing redux: when your A.I. Device asks: "What do you mean I'm not human?"

Business models depending on suckers to fork out cash for products and services... Fashion, haute cuisine, insurance & most start-ups.

Hey CFO, if you'd reduce all your reporting to ONE metric for the whole business, what would it be?

Yes, it's π day today. Or if you're lazy like me, you prefer July 22nd aka 22/7.

Constraints, by timeline;
10 to 5 yrs: willpower/ideas
5 to 2 yrs: money/assets
2 to 1 yr: regulation/process
<1 yr: ethics/pain

"Research from your desk" – Probably not where the action will be.

Innovation Manifesto: brings ambition and strategy to life. Not to be mistaken for its middle-mgmt alter ego, the Innovation Moanifesto.

Adding home delivery service to your inferior product doesn't compensate for the inferiority of your product.

Please stop referring to app development techniques when innovating in FMCG/CPG. Different worlds with very different rules.

Consider every change a threat, you'll end up a paranoid wreck. See it all as opportunity and you'll still go nuts, but you'll be more fun.

And just when you're about to make it to the top, the top moves. Again. Bugger.

Things we falsely believe make anyone money: discounts, QR Codes, digital start-ups, web-banners, Michelin stars, Amazon, royal estates.

**[What makes decisions "big"
is not the size of the options, but when
"not deciding" is no longer an option.]**

Nespresso: a story of 30 years of perseverance with a game changer, or just no one brave enough to kill it after 20 years of struggle?

Redefine your target category such that it scares you again. Comfort kills innovation.

[At innovation project briefing]
Researcher: "It's important to keep all this in mind."
Practitioner: "No it isn't."

The fallacy of pursuing a bad idea because too much effort has been sunk into it to let go. If you'd walk into it now, would you stay?

In order to understand the thing you love, you need to take distance from it. Like a Greek tragedy.

Trade drives cultural exchange faster than marriages ever can.

Health: you don't miss it until you lose it.
Ambition: you didn't miss it until you found it.

"I will simplify this, just to show I was involved" – when most things start getting too complicated.

Game Changers. That doesn't mean you need a dramatic new format. It means you need to remove a dramatic problem.

Market leader, copying the challenger is an embarrassing sign you've given up & lost the game.

Evolve what keeps you awake at night – move on to bigger scary things.

"Quick, get me your cheapest heart surgeon, fast!" – Management Fallacy.

In a sharing economy, what acronym will replace FMCG?

Hey CEO, the reality is that merely protecting what you have will *also* require changing it.

Bulletproof or Teflon coated?

Struggling to define an innovation ambition? Here's one, free of charge: DO THINGS THAT PISS OFF COMPETITION. You're welcome.

Prosperity grows from embracing change, paradoxically the one thing prosperous entities slowly grow out of embracing.

Zoom in on any business success story and you'll see it's merely that their successes outnumber their failures by one – the most recent one.

Driving consumer behaviour change? Or merely keeping up with shifting expectations? Please be realistic about your remit.

I hope the next food revolution will involve un-revolutionizing the previous ones a little.

Disrupt someone else's category before setting fire to your own. How? Consider any of your business capabilities and see how they'd translate into an advantage by switching your business between these domains;
- Consumer
- Professional
- Medical
- Travel
- Education
- Military

Chicken and Egg
"I need to know the strategy to create future ideas"
"I need to know future ideas to create a strategy""

'Crisis? What crisis?' – opportunity focused person

Entrepreneurship – Now there's a thing society can never have enough of.

If you want to know how good/bad your competition is doing, place fake job vacancy ads in their name.

Quick, what's the latest on FOMO!?

That moment you realize how growing fatter doesn't create new empty space for tattoos is EXACTLY the micro metaphor for how the universe expands.

Circular Economy: ask the Inuit for guidance, not Harvard professors.

[Paradox: If you pick a co-manufacturer over your own factory when you don't want to compromise, then you're setting yourself up for a long series of compromises.]

When you introduce 'The Next Best Thing', don't assume 'The Previous Best Thing' is just going to sit back and let you roll over them.

Client meeting location hierarchies
At your own office
Their CEO's Office
Fancy Restaurant
Hi-End virtual conferencing
Boardroom
Meeting Room
Communal Lounge
Procurement's Office
Client Canteen
Coffee Shop
Staged 'accidental' encounter at coffee machine
Car Park
Zoom/Teams
Phone
Email
Spam Folder

Follow the pain

WE INTRODUCED ANNOYING FLAWS IN THIS VERSION TO GIVE US SOME IMPROVEMENTS TO CELEBRATE IN NEXT YEAR'S NEW SERIES.

Follow the pain

Reveal real, unmet frustrations that will attract new customers to your innovative product or service. Too often innovation teams are distracted by industry truths and chasing generic trends or even common human needs. Whilst these are fun to investigate and keep everyone busy, their value for creating innovative and relevant new products and services is limited.

People will switch to your product only if it removes a functional or emotional frustration. C'est tout. In mature, saturated markets people will already be using a competitive product. Only their unhappiness there will drive a switch to your less frustrating alternative. Even in the dullest, most gridlocked markets there will be frustrations to resolve. The depth of the frustration you need to find is directly related to the business objective, in other words the innovation impact level you're looking to achieve. If it's merely snatching some customers away from your direct competition, resolving a small frustration will do. If you need to lure a whole new group of people away from another type of product and into your franchise, then you better find a big problem to solve for them or they'll just stay put where they are.

- Set the right scope and context to look for frustrations. This is basically a laddering exercise around the benefits that consumers enjoy from your product or portfolio. In case of a food product, is it taste, format, occasion, health, conviviality ... low down, you're comparing yourself with direct competition, splitting hairs over price, flavour and pack size. Consumers know how to judge your proposition, with a clear like-for-like assessment if you are truly resolving a frustration they are aware of. The higher up you go, the broader the competitive set of alternatives is, as well as the likelihood of having a strikingly different offer. But also equally less likely of being considered in the first place, nor it being clear why your offer would resolve a problem. Especially if your product is known for something completely differently. For example *"My yoghurt is the healthy indulgent outdoor snack!"* will need some explanation as there are plenty healthy OTG snacks already out there. The frustration might be a very nuanced version of health, while yoghurt isn't a product considered very portable in regular packaging. This is what *Blue Ocean Strategy*[1] boils down to, and worth the pain if the growth ambition is truthful.

- Know where to look, how to look and go beyond the obvious. A default information source for planning where to play is via U&A studies (Usage & Attitude). Besides them being expensive to commission, they're so focused on the narrow category definition you already operate in that you're not likely to find much value beyond what you already knew. Besides that, your direct competitors are using very similar research. And don't get me started on the quality of consumer panels in FMCG for this kind of investigation.

PRODUCT PLACEMENT

Get the *first* Grumpy book for an overview of shitty research sources.
Read the premise on page 176 now!

thoughts from a
GRUMPY
innovator

[1] *Check out the handy Innovation Glossary on page 156.*

Instead, consider using multiple sources, *especially* the newer ones like emotion analytics of consumer chatter online. Things people say when they're (un)happy enough to provide unprompted feedback. The gold dust of reviews.

- Whether informed qualitatively, quantitatively, once you made up your mind on the frustrations you will replace with excitement the trick is to progress to idea development asap. Don't waste time trying to prove the need is true. Proof comes from testing and trialing *ideas*, solutions.

All fashion trends rise and fall, except for tattoos which 'plateau'.

What is it with MacBook owners and that cloth they clamp inside? Neurotics.

Qual/quant consumer work – it's not meant to prove you're right. If you know you're right, skip all research and save money.

Are your products answering unmet needs or are you scaring your consumers into using them? Asking for a friend.

Understanding risk & path dependency: think of heavy drinking and using heavy machinery. In the right sequence, it's not a problem at all.

Set your research radars to 'super sensitive' if you want to chase noise all the time.

When you create a simplified model of a messy reality, the people using your model are unlikely to know what generalizations or simplifications you made. Your map will become their flawed cookie cutter reality.

I'm sorting & cleaning up my bookshelves and realize that I'd prefer to alphabetically sort my business books by title, and all the others by author.

All the coffees on my travel expense sheets are in fact cheap working space rentals. I tend to go for 1 coffee/hour/table.

**IT'S ALL CHOCOLATE, EVEN THE WINE GLASS.
APPARENTLY, *THIS* IS WHAT WOMEN REALLY WANT.**

I wonder if any of the world's millions of recorded helpdesk conversations actually ARE used for training purposes, or learning new things?

If you can move the masses, you only need to move them a little bit to create a proverbial tsunami. That's why most successful innovation and disruption is about resolving small frustrations for The Many, rather than big frustrations for The Few.

I don't think people change too much within their lifetime. But the societal norms around them of what's desirable or not shifts all the time.

Segmentation is in reality stereotyping, hard AF.

Market research and storytelling. Great, or awful things happen when combined. Handle with care, please.

Research Agencies spend fortune on shelf tracking & retail footfall analysis tools. Industry pundits cheer & applaud. Meanwhile, the audience shops online.

Of all the direct and indirect predictions that the Back To The Future series gave us, I'm still most puzzled by the manure dump truck.

Also, I'm now the same age as Christopher Lloyd was when he starred in the first Back to the Future movie: 47.

'I'm a celebrity get me outta here' – Millennials

Facts being counterintuitive > well, shit happens. Move on.

Intuition being counterfactual > shit will happen. Stop now.

I have a joke describing vegans, but really it's just facts and rather depressing.

On which page of your market research report should you reveal the outcomes?
A) 1
B) 10
C) 100
D) Suggest doing more research for proper answer.

Upgrade your segmentation research by calling it an Aristotlean investigation.

A map app for the moral high ground would automatically self-center.

To be brutally honest, I fear that for mainstream consumers Greta Thunberg is much less aspirational than Kim Kardashian.

Humans are LAZY. If you're looking to create behaviour change then remove a step from the process. Otherwise don't bother.

WELCOME TO OUR FOCUS GROUP.
TODAY WE ARE GOING TO TASTE MOLECULES.

I achieved peak-Taleb last week when I discovered my Kurdish barber also deadlifts.

Hey brand manager, don't go up into the stratosphere of emotional benefits and storytelling if your product/service isn't grounded by impeccable delivery.

'In my days [any activity] was so much more difficult' – older person talking, regardless of topic. And you know what kids? It's 100% true.

I wonder who Steve Jobs quoted on his own slides, when he was still alive?!

A whole industry was built around the insight that HOUSE and HOME are not the same thing. A similar principle underpins most other consumer markets.

I'm boarding a plane that is three seats wide, yet numbers them A, D and F. I find that quite presumptuous.

Can someone remind me which Myers-Briggs profiles have no sense of humour?

I have a joke about statistics, but $p<0.05$ you won't like it.

Every successful product in market will do well in tests[2]. But not every product you test successfully will do well in market.

Hey Marketing Manager, remember you are not a representative yourself of 98% of your consumers. You're *way* more pampered.

Being 'consumer centric' doesn't mean every business decision should be delegated to a focus group. On the contrary.

I can do 95% statistically confident research on toilet paper using the readers of this sentence. But 100% useless, as you're not really caring.

To everyone ignoring 50+ year olds as potential consumers... they hold 2/3 of the wealth and they actually have the time to shop for your stuff.
Also, a 87 year-old looks at a 62 year-old thinking: *'What a baby, my kid's age FFS'.*

Big idea for qual research facilities: put some exercise equipment in the back room, so you can get some workout done while listening.

---

[2] *Because respondents recognize it.*

Innovation for Millennials. It's a bit like looking for presents to buy for nephews and nieces whom you think are too spoiled already.

Husband: "Her qual research job is outta control"
Therapist: "What makes you think that?"
Wife [through mic behind mirror]: "Speak louder please"

Crude math, but heck: with less than 5% of innovation succeeding, you can see why 95% confidence levels in market research is 100% useless.

Before submitting yet another explorative piece of market research, ask yourself how much you can answer just by reading the newspapers.

If the question "What am I going to wear?" is top on your daily list of problems, you don't *really* have any problems. Cherish that.

Cosmetics insight: once you pass 40, your face takes twice as long to unwrinkle in the morning. And when camping, twice as long again.

In market research, a high 'N' is in fact a token of low confidence, not high. To a confident innovator, n~5 is more than enough.

Of all the reasons why innovation fails, "too little data" is seldom one.

My sons have discovered their safest bet for pizza is ordering variants that I don't like... THEY WON THAT BATTLE BUT THE WAR AIN'T OVER.

"We're going to need Bigger Data" – if Jaws were set in a market research department.

As long as Market Research refuses to reinvent itself as 'spotter of opportunity' rather than 'manager of risk', extinction for the industry looms. Soon.

[Remember your consumers would probably rather lose 10 pounds than gain 10 IQ points.]

Market Research Prizes That Should Exist
- Best Enabled Business Decision
- Most Accurate Prediction Of Actual Market Results
- Frustration spotted that inspired invention
- Stereotype-free segmentation study

Guys, are we all looking at the same Big Data? How many Big Datas are there? Is it not big enough by now to be just one big blobthing?

You won't attract many new consumers to your product's benefits if you don't alert them of the frustrations with their current product.

Automatic paper towel dispensers. Is it me, or are they simply not generous enough?

YES IT'S EXPENSIVE FOR AN N=1 FOCUS GROUP, BUT IS THIS QUALITY FEEDBACK OR WHAT?!

"The more data you collect, the more you can;
A) Identify conflicts
B) Cherry-pick
Research is intrinsically about building stories.

A: "... But is this where you lost your keys?"
B: "No, but at least here there's enough light to see"
Analogy for most market research

Insisting your volume of research makes your business on average smarter is like saying psychiatrists on average make smarter life choices.

If you think of your respondents like consultants... would you then still prefer to listen to n=200 average ones, instead of n=3 good ones?

It appears "you guys" is slowly creeping into the English language as replacement for "you" in 2nd person plural. And it sounds awful."

The significance of whatever makes you happy shouldn't correlate too much to the amount of happiness you already have, right?

Make any quant researcher nervous by insisting they divulge their source of data, ie the skewed, bribed panel they call 'respondents'.

The diet product sweet spot: are you more peckish than you are active.
The beauty product sweet spot: you are more vain than you are confident.
The convenience product sweet spot: you are lazier than you are stingy.

Interact with consumers to understand their frustrations and what's really going on.
Not to make decisions for you; that's *your* job.

Judging by the gargantuan size of most market research reports, I think "Big Data" refers to the output, not the size of input.

If your quant research supplier is explaining how you can achieve higher scores, he/she is only explaining how to beat their own algorithms.

A: "You know your BigGreenEgg® is just a snob's barbecue, right?"
B: "It's not snobbery, I just prefer the flavour of smoked over grilled."

High stress workforces in cramped, tiny spaces: Leopard tank unit, Apollo 13, Greek trireme slave galley and Caffé Nero at LCY Airport.

How far a walk is it?
Is it like only LHR5 A7>A21 far, LCY G22>G7 far, AMS H7>B28 far, or f-ng FRA Z11>A2 far?

"SIX guilders for a coffee you bought out of mere boredom while waiting for a train?!?!" – My 1992 self, disagreeing with my 2018 behaviour.

Hey futurologist, your sleeve tattoos kinda undermine your credibility for long term vision, no?

I spent all evening speaking with UK women about chocolate and now I'm wondering if I should feel surprised, enlightened or disturbed.

Processed Foods.
aka French cuisine.

My insight from all our work in 'home cooking' from this past year: the real threat isn't from new ways of cooking, but not cooking at all.

Once you have a hypothesis, data transforms into evidence. Otherwise it's just words & numbers.

A: "Plz recruit users of product X and Y"
B: "We can't, incidence is too low :-("
A: "OK, only X users then"
Hope flies out of window

The real reason many marketers prefer quant research over test launches, even at the lower cost and speed, is you can't cheat in test launches.

"Consumer Co-creation" – the methodology that created classics like The Edsel, New Coke, The Millennium Dome, BK Crispy Fries and Boaty McBoatface.

Show me a consumer who asks for 'disruption' and I'll show you an anarchist maniac. The word doesn't mean to them what it means to you.

There comes a point your research iterations are so close together you're just chasing noise, not a signal.

If you know the viewing facility's food menu by heart, it's time to move to another research methodology, not another venue.

Looking to commission an 'infographic' to sauce up your data? Make sure the designer actually understands the data or it'll just be a mess.

Decisions should eventually be based on n=1. The 1 being the person who deals with the consequences.

Rate how much you love your partner on a Lickert scale and you'll find that:
1) Lickert scales don't work
2) It's a little creepy too

Meta-question: will a survey among n=1,000 market researchers reveal the true state of the market research industry? I'm not so sure.

"Mirror Mirror on the wall, who's the prettiest of them all?" – Focus group viewing rooms, every day.

Focus group viewing facilities ... where people on both sides of the mirror pretend they care.

Twice the amount of data will also give you twice the amount of conflicting data.

While your shopper- and consumer-insights-manager bicker over who owns that part of the journey, your real audience switches to competition.

I had a project conversation about Xylitol that was so passionate I think there's good material for a musical in there.

To the teams developing all these new market research tools: without improving the shoddy underlying respondent panels, it's like developing fancy apps for BlackBerry OS.

Successful writers do not "co-create" books with their readers. So when co-creating with consumers, know your role & responsibility vs theirs.

"We can't possibly make our product premium :-(" – says Marketing Manager, then takes a sip from a $3/250ml bottle of water.

'Specialist' doesn't mean 'very good' or 'expert'. it means 'narrow focus'. Keep that in mind when picking your job title, or hiring specialists.

Wife: "His job in market research is taking over our marriage."
Therapist: "Sir, what do you have to say about that?"
Husband: "Typical over-indexing for her Extravert Controller persona."

[Candy packaging paradox: fun size is the least fun.]

Mansplaining sports injuries by 40+ year old males: "Clearly, my gear wasn't expensive enough. And I need more of it".

*** SPOILER ALERT ***
The moment Millennials have children, they become as square as every generation before them. Maybe even squarer."

"Total Addressable Market" – Interesting definition for postal logistics companies and internet dating.

Only market researchers can get away with outright discriminatory statements about segmentation, lead users & hi-relevance consumers.

Wife: "He's only interested in numbers, thinks in-the-box, always late and I can't rely on his advice" BFF: "Leave him. It's a Usage & Attitude problem"

Swiping an iPhone as wireless clicker for a PowerPoint presentation? About as pompous as saying 'next slide' to your Google Glasses.

On fancy food ingredients. Be aware that many people think a calorie is an ingredient, and full-fat milk is 100% fat. Etcetera ignorance.

Funny how young kids think milk is made in the supermarket, while we all know it's made by home delivery companies.

"Optimism Bias" – what gets difficult stuff done.

Qual vs Quant, aka Opinions vs Statistics.
Both are bendable, subjective & fallible.

The Bored act in mysterious ways.

Things with no value are seldom free.

Sadly, it's far more difficult to build a case on your deep understanding of consumers, than on a direct quote from some random person in the street.

"Let your gut guide you, not the guide gut you." – Mohammed Ali's focus group moderator friend.

"Island Time" – A mindset, independent of topography or time.

Science is about proving you're wrong, Market Research is about proving you're right. Not the same, sorry.

Hey Gen-X, wondering why Millennials are so odd? Then just imagine what you'd have done to fight the boredom taking 10 more years to grow up.

"Take me to your leader." – trend spotter

KnockKnock
Who's there?
Semi
Semi Who?
Semi Monadic
KnockKnock KnockKnock KnockKnock KnockKnock
KnockKnock KnockKnock KnockKnock

Logging on through Citrix ... you just know the software on the other side is not going to deliver an enjoyable user experience.

The fact you are a Regular/Heavy User of toilet paper doesn't mean you have interesting opinions about it. Lapsed Users on the other hand...

NPS survey reports sound like cheesy dating shows.

"Sharing Economy" ... is that Millennial-speak for being broke?

If you want to understand the different in digital privacy laws between the US, Europe and China, just visit a local public toilet.

Passing between me and my luggage is like walking between Mama Bear and her cubs.

Jackson Pollock was so ahead of his time: just look at his Big Data infographics as early as the 1940's.

How do you best treat an anomaly in your research?
A) Explain with fuzzy statistics
B) Kill with fire
C) Celebrate

[Archive reports don't talk back, nor get angry when you disagree with them. That's why they're way too comfortable for using as sole base for your work.]

If you don't believe disgust and desire can go hand in hand... imagine the person next to you on the train eating a kebab.

As a rule of thumb, presume your consumers care about 95% less about your products than you do. Just to manage expectations.

The problem with having too much data is that you feel extra stupid not to be able to make sense of it.

Personality tests. Remind me again which Myers-Briggs type was the one that doesn't get sarcasm?

Last week's Fortnite championships show the coming of age of Generation Z, the watershed moment that Millennials realize they can join us Gen-X'ers in the league of irrelevant 'has beens'.

PPTs: Very Nar-row text-box-es are a nuis-ance to read Please choose smal-ler font size or wide-n box. Thank you.

Lickert scales in market research can be simplified to a Y/N question: 'is this badass or not?' Seriously, excitement is all you need.

Isn't it incredible how Generation-Z is stealing Millennials' limelight with genuinely nicer interests? Sustainability and saving the planet, rather than gastro-burgers and selfies. There is hope for mankind.

Your response to fresh snow reveals your mental age.

Remember that only 3-4 years ago, our biggest concern was whether we were hydrated enough.

In business data analysis ... flashy analysis is used to mask poor quality data. Good data speaks for itself.

Heuristic: never take dietary advice from anyone under 40. Make that 50.

Trend agencies regurgitate selectively from the past. If they could predict the future, they'd be the richest businesses ever. They're not.

Eye Tracker MR: "I will allow researchers to post-rationalize design decisions ad infinitum"
Neuro MR: "Hold my beer"

People do not want to be 'educated' about the tech enabling your product. Just like you don't want to be educated about things like motor oil and pet insurance.

Sometimes a stock photo says more than a 1,000 words. But it usually just says “stock photo”.

Dear FMCG innovation person, please don't forget to use your own products every now and then, even if you're not the target audience. Tool Wag Dog.
Aka Methodolorgy.

If you do Market Research only to convince internal stakeholders, you'd better just spend that money on wining, dining or bribing them.

Can someone remind me which Myers-Briggs profiles tend to blow the family fortune? Or was it a nurture/nature thing?

There is broooaaad grey area between an attempt to make technology exciting for the masses and tapping a pool of gullible nerds who buy everything.

Logic and narrative form our stories of our Past, and musings about our Future. Yet in transit through the Now, they temporarily vanish.

Given the peculiar position in which many people hold their phones nowadays, I suggest phone designers look at pizza slices for inspiration.

The ancient Greeks identified 4 personality types, fully intertwined with environment. Farmers, City people, Warriors and Mountain people. Because they understood context and character are indivisible.

The Salmon. Aka the person disembarking from a plane who first needs to fetch hand luggage from bin at higher seat row.

I estimate that 87.3% of statistics present a false level of accuracy.

Sometimes the Bull's Eye Consumer is so specific they're even less likely to exist than the Perfectly Average Consumer.

My sons' maths and fractions skills improve dramatically when I apply it to how much of their pizza I want to claim.

IF THIS IS YOUR SHELF DISPLAY
YOU NEED CHOPPER INSIGHT

Maybe we need more Consumer Segment Personas?" – Such a typical Stressed Structure Seeker thing to say.

BAR MENU

== TODAY'S CHEESY SPECIALS ==

[A Procurement Manager walks into a bar]
"I want a discount on my beer!"
"No problem."
[Barman serves smaller beer]

[A man walks into a Bay Area Start-up Bar]
"I'd like 2,500 free craft beers please."
"Sure, if you Instagram them."
[Barman sells bar for $200m]

[Risk Analyst walks into a bar]
"You know you're risking your health here, right?"
"You know you're risking yours saying that here, right?"
[Business continues as normal]

[The Bar franchise CEO plans tour of the premises]
[Barman tidies up bar, wipes tables & kicks out drunk patrons]
CEO: "See? Our bars look nice."

[An operations analyst walks into a bar]
"If you pre-fill your beer glasses in the daytime lull, you'll achieve a 30% better tap utilization during evening rush hour"
[Patrons leave and bar goes out of business]

[A Marketing Persona walks into a bar]
"I want an experience that fits my mood."
"Are you an Extravert Optimizer or so?"
[Orders same beer as everyone else]

[A market researcher walks into a bar]
"I'm here to find the truth"
"We're here to forget the truth"
[Writes report on Millennials instead]

[A Six Sigma Black Belt walks into a bar]
"Whatever you're doing, you're doing it all wrong."
"Fuck off"
[Everyone orders another drink & life goes on]

[An Early Adopter walks into a bar]
"You do accept Bitcoins, right?"
"No."
[Orders six-pack on Amazon Prime and drinks at home, alone]

Make It Worth The Trouble

IF YOU WORK FOR FREE, I INVEST ZERO AND WE LAUNCH TWO YEARS AGO... WE MIGHT JUST MAKE ENOUGH TO HIT OUR TARGETS.

Make It Worth The Trouble

The theory is easy. Leverage your capabilities across the marketing mix, staying close to home for innovation designed to protect existing business, and go wild when a more disruptive impact is aspired.

Creating products that consumers love in tests is easy: just give them what they want. Creating products they love and make money for you is a different matter. Success is then defined by the degree to which you can use your current people, capabilities and assets. If you're looking to create a new product to launch next year to nudge a competing brand out of the way, then your current manufacturing assets will likely be the limiting factor. So you need to find a way to answer the consumer frustration you found, with solutions that you can make in your factory now. If you're looking to create longer term innovations to open up a new audience of consumers in another aisle in the supermarket, then your sales team's capability to build new customer relationships might well be the limiting factor you need to work within.

To succeed, one has to understand and acknowledge what the limiting factors will be to achieve success. Crudely summarized:

- For renovation and close-in innovation, your existing assets are the limiting factor; be it manufacturing, brand, channel dependence etcetera. Simply because you have neither the time, nor the likely ROI to commit to anything expensive or complicated. Create ideas accordingly.
- For more dramatic innovation aimed at attracting new consumers and drive growth, your organizational structure, capability and culture will more likely be the

constraint. But the likely returns much higher and your timeline is probably set accordingly.

The problem isn't this theory, but that many businesses either don't acknowledge their constraints, or want their cake and eat it. To some degree, this is pure optimism bias at work. But there is a darker side, which is that in many FMCG businesses the organizational structure and KPI's have been stacked against succeeding.

In many FMCG businesses, responsibility for innovation has shifted to Marketing and Consumer Insight teams. The reason of course being to get to a smarter, more consumer centric portfolio. Which is fabulous. But the possible downside is serious.

- Firstly, Marketers seldom have a background in R&D or Operations, which means they seldom truly understand how their products are made, misjudge feasible versus affordable and find out too late what really can be done at what cost. In the quick-response context of renovation, they might be lured to copying what they see competitors do, ignorant that they might be working off completely different technology. To make matters worse, with Marketing at the innovation helm, it's also in the hands of people with the fastest career churn in the business.
- With innovation responsibility and influence seeping away from R&D and Operations, their role is basically reduced cost optimization: "Just make it cheap". That mindset is corrosive, not because it's a bad but because it's addictive. An engineer will take great pride from squeezing cost out that no consumer notices.[3] And that

[3] *Eventually, they notice. Salami slicing never goes unpunished.*

mindset spreads and becomes the starting point for any request coming in, including new innovation. And in order to make something new at the best cost, you need the newest production kit. Old lines are written off too soon, and the volumes promised to cover investing in the new ones never come.

- When the relationship between the innovation defining and creation forces are disturbed as above, the business innovative capability spirals downward. Marketers push to outsourcing NPD production and lose tremendous margin, whilst manufacturing assets lie idle that could have crafted a much higher margin alternative albeit not as cheaply as current cash cows.

Effectively innovating businesses are insight-led and asset-out in their work, especially in renovation and mid-term innovation. They join up the demand and supply functions that make ideas work commercially.

Meanwhile in the domain of disruptive innovation, things have changed dramatically (no pun intended). In the mid-2010's, a new problem surfaced in many FMCG businesses: category growth plateau'd or even declined. While at the same time digital companies were growing sky high. Within a very short time span, this ignited FMCG boardroom belief that the innovation and development models used in software would unlock the same growth. Enter the Lean Start-up, the Incubator, Agile working, etcetera.

The premise was in fact very good: idea development with lots of experimentation, iteration with many prototypes. Launching and immediately improving, testing in market. It's good stuff, especially for driving breakthrough outputs. But Silicon Valley's new ways of working had a spell-binding impact on FMCG innovation functions, I suspect because the people involved would rather have work ed for a startup than a blue chip.

Five years down the line, Goliath organizations adopting David's nifty little tools have gotten themselves in a bit of trouble.

- The heralded start-ups run on different business models, with market land-grab being the main driving force objective and making a profit much less relevant. Blue chips cannot afford this.
- Many corporate incubators are sponsored entirely by a single function, e.g. Marketing. The connection to the rest of the organization is weak. When a startup does make it through to a scaleup stage, the essential support from other functions isn't there, nor rooted in shared KPI's.
- So many blue-chip incubators are working on ideas simply too small to be of interest to the mothership. Products that appear exciting and breakthrough are often quite niche. Even if they would fulfill their maximum potential in 2-3 years (say, 10's of millions revenue), they will likely still be a complete mismatch to the blue chip's requirements: 100's of millions revenue, global impact, etc. Much would be won by ruthlessly culling incubators based on true potential: only small bets, only with big potential upside.

Like with the Old Skool reality of needing to marry insight & manufacturing, the Nu Skool world has its own reality that needs acknowledging: Blue Chips are good at *scaling*, not crafting from scratch. A more successful interpretation in this reality seems to be M&A. Spot and buy the small business with the winning disruption when they're still small, adapt for mass, and then scale up.
Bingo.

Do not project onto your customers your lazy desire to keep brand & features unchanged on the premise of them wanting 'iconic' experiences.

The positioning alphabet runs from 'A' to 'THE'.

Is there AI to detect bad taste? Probably not, for it's impossible to calibrate.

Always remember that Nature has more things that can kill you than can heal you.

Hey Engineer; you could do a full Failure-Mode-And-Effects-Analysis on your design, OR you just ask my mother to panic over all its dangers.

Simplicity implies deconstruction, then reduction, to retain whatever core matters.

2010 Food innovators at work:
"Leek" – nah
"Broccoli" – nope
"Spinach" – too 1930's Popeye
"Kale" – yuck
"Onion" – makes my eyes water. Wait, go back one?

Can we agree not to refer to start-ups as 'successful' until they reach at least some kind of breakeven? Before then, the jury's still out.

Is it me, or has Tell Sell reinvented itself as the Instagram ad feed? Seriously, it's a non-stop barrage of useless crap.

MARKETING ASKS IF YOU CAN MAKE THE AROMA EXPERIENCE MORE 'EXTRAVERT' AND 'SPIRITUAL'.

What is the marketing/sales term for the following discrepancy?
- CD Players cost $250
- DVD Players that can play CD's & 20 other formats are $50

UX Designer: 'So it's better to do one click 1000 times, than 1000 clicks only once?'
Bruce Lee: 'I said kicks and that's not what I meant'

Hotel light switch designers come from the same design schools as hotel shower control designers. The design school of shit.

Once you experience that viability, not creativity is innovation's main challenge, you immediately appreciate Creators over Creatives more.

The urge to simplify all concepts to 'single benefit/minded' was driven by comms and research, not by people creating or buying products.

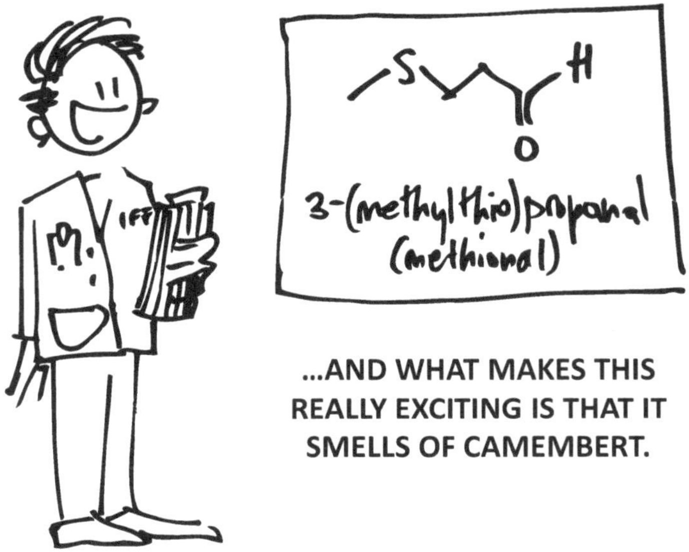
S
H
O
3-(methylthio)propanal
(methional)
...AND WHAT MAKES THIS REALLY EXCITING IS THAT IT SMELLS OF CAMEMBERT.

Consumer goods innovators everywhere are adopting Agile and running sprints, just like in software development. Fine, but has anyone broken them the news yet this is followed by endless rounds of debugging?

"Hey, my cousin Tony can get me a great deal on shuttle trains." – Design team meeting, planning Seattle Tacoma Airport.

There should be a Hippocratic oath for product designers, pledging not to kill their users.

Full of emotion, I typed ""(:*,') +_!!!"" and hit send. Then realized "thank you!!" with alt- instead of shift- doesn't communicate well.

It's much easier to show 'craft' by working from a low benchmark than a high one. Gourmet hamburgers vs winning a second Michelin star.

Yellow Sharpies... Why? Discuss.

'What problem are we solving here?' #ForgottenInnovationQuestions

My new noise cancelling headphones are great for flights, they completely cancel out the applause of the tourists on board.

A start-up in “pre-revenue phase” is a hypothesis, not a business.

Is it me, or are architects very arrogant when it comes to their buildings' inhabitants suggesting other ways of using their creations?

I found email spam a lot friendlier when it was just about penis enlargements. Now it's a daily barrage of phishing scams.

Contains Ascorbic acid. EEEW
Contains Preservative. EEEW!
Contains Vitamin C. YAAAY!!
... How to push-pull with only one ingredient."

Which is the most compelling benefit; Comfort or Pain Management?

You just know a prototype test is going to be fantastic if you're given goggles, earplugs, a helmet and are then asked to stand back a bit.

True craftmanship: when there are no layers between someone's actions and the beautiful result of those actions.

"Maybe we should invent a new word to describe this new idea of ours?" – The moment a bad idea gets worse.

[Stevia. My brain gets it, my taste buds don't.]

Why not try LESS 'user experience' to improve your product/service, rather than more?

Movie pitch 'Food Science, The Musical'
Nutritionist discovers new superfood berries but Evil EFSA auditor forbids claims. Fight in court, fall in love when they realize it's only the taste that matters.
The End.

— · — · — · — · — · — ·

Movie pitch 'The Ladder'
Man frustrated in corporate job, barrier to promotion proves frustrating, then discovers hierarchy is only a figure of imagination.
The End.

— · — · — · — · — · — ·

Movie pitch 'The Freelancer'
Made redundant, woman makes discovery that 'Unemployed, begging for work' and 'Liberated looking for fun work' are the same thing.
The End.

— · — · — · — · — · — ·

Movie pitch 'Cash Flow Jungle'
Start-up founder fails to find seeding capital. Decides to bootstrap, retain 100% ownership and grow organically instead, lives happily ever after in great wealth.
The End.

Today I learned the word "Floccinaucinihilipilification", which means "the action or habit of estimating as worthless".

"Is it simply glorious?" – would be fine by me as idea selection criterium. It's also surprisingly binary: you can't have a somewhat glorious idea.

The only people more annoyingly in-my-way at airports than tourists, are tourists' extended family dropping them off or picking them up.

Over-simplified problem statements elicit over-simplified solutions.

These poor start-up founders nowadays, they're just tooo busy. Like having to go meet other start-up founders at conferences three times a week. Back in the old days we only had to focus on our clients.

I probably had a Soylent-equivalent diet during my student years, but what if I'd continued in the 25 years since?

I believe one and the same company developed the US market for cubicles and public toilets.

Try explaining a Mb/Gb data plan to anyone under 35 and you realize they were never really restricted by things like floppy disks, bandwidth, finite storage.

**[Union Jack:
My preferred Pritt stick pattern.]**

Think of Artificial Intelligence like artificial sweeteners. Once hailed as the future of humanity but held back by the odd aftertaste.

Airline oxygen mask: "please note the bag does not inflate". FFS WHY NOT MAKE IT SUCH THAT DOES INFLATE AND NO ONE PANICS?!

'YOU'RE DOING IT ALL WRONG' – UX designers at testing labs yelling at the respondents.

New XBox console will run at 12 Teraflops, roughly level with the world's supercomputers in 2001. Somehow I had thought there would be less than19 years difference. Nevertheless, imagine the Cray team sneaking in a game of Call Of Duty while downloading the latest Janet Jackson.

I just switched on a heater in a hotel room where the air conditioning can't be switched off. I'm expecting rain & a Greenpeace raid in here soon.

Why haven't travel agencies repositioned their Single's holidays as Selfie Holidays yet? You're missing a trick here, guys.

Lack of creativity is not the reason you're not successfully innovating. It's your capability to be creative within business constraints.

A: "What kind of tech interests you?"
B: "The kind of tech that only makes a sound when I drop it."

Idea not good enough yet? Add the prefix "Natural", "3D Printed", "Gluten-Free", "IoT-Connected", "VR-Enabled" or "Graphene". Hey presto!

Two half-baked ideas do no count as one fully baked one.

Her: "You don't understand my needs!"
Him: "Just tell me what you want!?"
Her: "You should know!"
Him: "Be specific please!"
[Marketing + R&D]

Add 'gamification' to commoditized services and you'll make them more cumbersome, not more fun.

"It's the winning idea!" – Statement from someone yet to discover the difference between potential and actual impact.

Humans are primarily fear driven creatures, as a creative consequence we're much better at brainstorming for problems than we are solutions.

It seems most creativity techniques assume you need to be uncomfortable to work outside your comfort zone. How stupid.

[Most people asking for more ideas simply need fewer better ones.]

"I want more leather!" – Car interior designer who needs less plastic first.

Would the team who created Panavision Ultrawide screens appreciate that 60 years later, most videos are in Ultra Narrow Portrait format?

Good improvisation is based on experience. Which makes it more of a memory effort than a creative effort.

[Giving tour of our house]
Mouth: "And that's my son's LEGO."
Brain: "My LEGO. All mine."

Graveyard for failed bike-sharing start-ups, Hangzhou, China

MAN, UR A VISIONARY!

I suspect that financially successful artists find their inspiration in business books.

If you systematically manipulate concepts to pass a database driven hurdle, then you're filling your database with fabricated concepts.

Will car brands' self-driving algorithms follow their stereotypes?
Alfa Romeo: anti-social
BMW: speeding
Peugeot: at 75% of speed limit
Hummer: too close behind
Fiat: One gear too low

Is there a question imaginable where the answer is: "You need more tattoos"?

**Tinkering Excel sheets versus tinkering prototypes ...
Two worlds that seldom meet.**

If your consumers knew what % of the price they're paying is for funding the "amazing-shelf-presence" pack vs the product inside, they'd not buy it.

Storage byte sizes are 1,000's times more now than they were 25 years ago. Also the OralB® brush timing app is 76Mb, so overall no progress.

Ergonomics being taught at Industrial Design courses is a bit cynical if students end up working in passenger airplane seat design.

Just like in the movies, in innovation projects it's stunt doubles doing the heavy lifting for the movies stars who take home the prizes

160/[AGE] = Number of hours you can sleep comfortably on an inflatable camping mattress.

[Positioning: don't describe what it is, but how it's different.]

Do not overestimate what technology can accelerate or simplify. My case: e-Passport customs control.

Is there a name for the future moment that digital consumer cameras surpass the resolution of Kodak Ektachrome? Or has it already happened?

Remember: improving is one thing, inflating another.

There's a reason no one has yet invented homeopathic laundry detergent, and it's not because of the dirty laundry.

Funny how creative gurus working in innovation truly believe and insist that creativity is the only problem preventing successful innovation.

Nowadays true 'smartness' can only be judged by how well a device performs when disconnected from the internet. Same for people, by the way.

I drove a car through Naples and came out al dente.

I presented two webinars to 100 innovators and I told one half there's always a good solution, the other half there's always a good problem.

Anyone reducing people's trust in household remedies as 'superstition' isn't acknowledging what drives trust in today's modern solutions.

Disappointed there are things you simply cannot 'accelerate' or 'fast-track'? Just giving them more attention will do fine too.

Tip. Pre-heat your coffee cups with a coffee beforehand. You're welcome.

Crudely paraphrasing Robert Capa: "If your ideas aren't good enough, you're not close enough."

Fact: if you cycle through rain long enough, capillary action drives water up via your socks, trousers into your underpants. I have proof.

Hey tourist, do you wear that silly plastic poncho at home too, when it rains? Just asking.

[I think some creative agencies would do well to assign an Uncreative Director, to counterbalance some of the fluff they generate.]

If your take on innovation is chasing flavours of the day, instead of genuine progress, then you'll always remain fragile to competitors' flavour updates.

Beauty transcends the sum of parts, which is why there is often beauty where parts are missing.

Every new encounter with experienced innovators starts with exchanging war stories and showing scars. Physical scars, in particular.
"...and then that gasket that couldn't blow, did.""

[Tweeting after nice concert]
Thank you Radishes.
Fuck you Autocorrect.
Thank you Radiohead.

Sometimes a stock photo says more than a 1,000 words. But it usually just says 'stock photo'.

Again, I witness one of innovation's great miracles, an idea that sounds stupid but for peculiar reasons works: easyJet Speed Boarding.

Murphy's Law is only a problem for those who can't fix things.

[Every successful new idea will have passed through multiple stages of being a bad one.]

A self-driving motorcycle. Now THAT would be scary.

Hey marketers, it's good product your consumers will come back for, not more storytelling.
No product, no repeat.

Engineering, like music, reveals the fundamental beauty of ideas with a purpose.

"Stay calm, count to #FF" – a Javascript coder losing patience.

Just spoke with a client who moved from Switzerland to France, and all the hassle such transition brings. Like going from QWERTY to AZERTY.

Just a note to confirm New Jersey is the best place for consumer work on Xylitol. Because pronunciation.

Borrow with pride
– and keep your lawyer on speed dial.

"Internet of Things". Aka the belief that two commoditized, stupid devices can have a meaningful conversation.

Every touch-point on a customer journey is a touch-point too many. Journeys with less steps always win. TOUGH LUCK, UX DESIGNER.

"Is it good quality?"- Close eyes, mentally fast-forward 10 years of operation, open eyes. Still OK? Works for products, buildings & people.

Great Packaging drives trial, great Product drives repeat.

Workshops... there's always ONE person who insists on writing their post-its in portrait rather than of landscape orientation.

Billion dollar idea: Q-tips you ARE allowed to stick in your ears. FFS

Proof that owning good domain names beats trademarks is in the silly trademarks that are being registered nowadays to pair with domains.

Your product is merely an obstacle between your consumer/user and what benefit they want from the product. Fewer layers in between is always better.

Does your organization have MBA's as so-called guardians for innovation to keep the creatives in check? Show me the successes that brought.

Hey service designer. Remember your service is a means to an end, not the end itself. The less steps/clicks/calls, the better.

SEARCH(String$("Happiness");Area$(CITRIX))=FALSE

** SPOILER ALERT ** Optimizing concept copy in accordance to Quant supplier suggestions helps you beat their database, not the real market.

[The difference between Design and Engineering is the level of bullshit you can get away with.]

The best thing in bread since sliced bread turns out to be non-sliced bread. Go figure, Progress.

Somewhere, someone has a full-time job undoing what you do full-time for a living. Yet you both go to work every day, feeling productive.

Whatever you consider as 'packaging design' will be considered by your end consumer as UN-packaging design. You assemble, they disassemble.

Intelligence comes in shades, which goes for Artificial Intelligence too.
- Paranoid AI email filter
- Comforting AI Customer Service chatbot
- Conservative stock market AI advisor
- Reckless self-driving AI controls
- Cooking app with sweet tooth AI

I refuse to say 'OK Google' to my phone, and just tap instructions instead. Is that my introvert nature or am I just old fashioned?

'I store my stuff in the Cloud' rings differently than
'I save my files on one of Google's servers in Atlanta.'

After another 25 years of gorging on hipster burgers and cane sugar macarons, Millennials of 2040 will undoubtedly launch organic insulin shots.

'MUHAHAHA FOOLS!' – What I think every time someone offers voluntarily to have their hand luggage placed in the hull.

Character in Lord Of The Rings, Or Decorative Paint Brand?

Valspar	Jotachar	Betolux Akva
Wijzonol	Glidden	Owatrol
Finngard	Alphaxylan	Jotun Treolje
Miranol	Tikkurila	Wilcombe Cotton
Rubbol	Amphibolin	Vorlack
Haftgrund	Histolith	Hempadur

The new Marvel harder-than-diamond superhero. Part Man, Part Buckminster-Fuller Graphene.

On the increase of non-medicinal brands considering cannabis as ingredient.
1) Make propositions for multi-person consumption.
2) Include something edible like peanut butter sandwiches"

Electric car designers should look at storing energy in on-board trays of lasagna, that stuff stays frigging hot forever.

Gen-X: 'Topic_Date_Author_Version.doc, 744Kb'
Gen-Y: 'Hangry Final Final REV6.pptx, 125Mb'
Gen-Z: 'LOL.mp4, 2.4Gb'"

Does Tesla's anti-collision algorithm allow for certain exemptions? Asking for a friend.

After your concept fails in testing, should you...
A) Blame writer
B) Blame researcher
C) Blame respondents
D) Retest until it passes"

I have the impression we're shifting from an addiction to oil, to an addiction to electricity.

NOW MOVE FFS

I UNDERSTAND IT'S READY TO GO AND YOUR TEAM IS WAITING, BUT LET'S RE-CUT THAT POWERPOINT A COUPLE MORE TIMES AND GET A FEW MORE PEOPLE TO WEIGH IN. ALSO, WE NEED LINE OF SIGHT ON THE Y3 VOLUME FORECAST WITH A LITTLE MORE GRANULARITY.

OH AND THE SALES SVP HAD A GOOD POINT, I THINK...

NOW MOVE FFS

Paralysis, inertia and utter cowardice are perhaps the most underlit reason for innovation programs grinding to a halt. The act of keep the momentum through all layers of decision-making, without letting 'risk-aversion' get in the way, is undeniably a tremendous effort. And that's not surprising, as the typical corporate innovation stage gate is designed to stop ideas from passing, rather than lovingly developing them.

I suspect a significant part of the capability to act on an innovative idea, the willingness to back it and move to action, is rooted at the very beginning of the journey. Is the business objective of the innovation understood, and has the route to creating a solution been pegged at the right level of impact. Incremental tweaks in accordance to category norms for small objectives, or bold idea shored by smart experiments and proof points for a big ambition. Both ends of the spectrum obviously carry their particular risk/reward balance, and if incorrectly matched it will surely feel like a bad idea. Especially to a decision making committee who need to decide based on hearsay, e.g. a PowerPoint presentation. If the business syntax describing risk/reward in innovation isn't clear, then amount of misunderstanding and backtracking will make every innovation project a long, long slog to work through.

It seems that in large corporate environments, there are two product launches to work through. The internal one, with a slow ramp-up of momentum, and then the real-world one. And where you want the external launch to be big and brash, you want the internal one as small and nimble as possible.

Engage internal & external stakeholders accordingly, such that they will invest in turning your ideas into reality. The impact levels make the difference. Protect-level innovation initiatives are often small improvements that can be planned by the calendar by a single team. Keep senior management far away. The other two levels, innovation for growth or disruption, need a harmonious business ecosystem to survive. Grow-level is truly opportunity-led and will require collaboration between disciplines to create new standards. Transformational innovation requires a bold vision and even bolder personality to push it through. But across all three, an energized business climate is required to keep innovative ideas intact through to the end – developing them positively, not compromising them and losing sight of the business objective that ignited the process in the first place. Create metrics for every stage gate that drive love into the ideas, and strengthening them through incremental improvement, not culling.

In this context of driving innovative ideas through a business to a successful launch, there is often mention of an entrepreneurial mindset. What appears often misunderstood is what the entrepreneur's mindset means when it comes to innovation in large organizations. Because you don't want entrepreneurs – they are wild, undomesticated and need the real world to rumble and tumble in to figure out what works. The 'intraprenurial' mindset that works in a large corporate ecosystem is different. They have the skills to look at ideas through the lens of the business structure, the framework that needs to be 'played' to go from idea to launch. Which is much more about knowing who to convince with what, than just figuring out a good product idea. They are the slightly rebellious team members and likely have no interest in being an entrepreneur outside in the wild. They love their employer and their jobs; and they are eager to stretch the current operational straitjacket into a new shape. The more dramatic the change required the more excited they get, not because they know exactly what to do, but because they know they can make it right. They exist in every organization, in every function and are the opposites of the operational excellence people. They dislike structure and love ambiguity – just what you need to figure out how to get new things done successfully.

Corporate intrapreneurs, the rebels are resourceful to the point of being Machiavellian. With the difference being they battle for the survival of the idea. They know how to engage with internal and external stakeholders such that they will invest their skin in turning a concept into reality.

oking back at the chapters before, and wondering how to end my tips & tricks about the journey to launch with a bang – I realize there isn't really one. Though perhaps there is one cliché to be brought back into the spotlight.

TRUST.

I'm typing this on August 22nd 2020. Tomorrow is my 24th anniversary of my graduation as an Industrial Design Engineer. In all those years of working in product innovation, I have never seen a team work through to a successful launch of any kind without a solid foundation of trust among them. Only *trust* allows teams to work with ambiguous criteria, with the liberty to figure things out when they (inevitably) don't always work out as planned. Trust is what moves people , and ideas to thrive. No score cards, no manifestos, no brand KPI's can ever create that drive to push ideas through, big or small.

So... No magic ingredients, It's all about good cooking.

Behind this successful product, there is the story of someone who believed in the opportunity and pushed and pushed and pushed and then should have failed except for this case study.

Moderate Coffee Consumption" is 25 cups a day right? Asking for a friend.

Reminder: REDUCING RISK ALSO REDUCES LUCK. Remember there's no success story without some luck involved.

A: 'Awesome, are you playing Tetris?!'
B: 'FU. This is my calendar weekday view. :-(

Is time damaging, or strengthening?
[Insert hockey stick curve]

Never agree to a shorter timeline without also agreeing where you're allowed to cut corners, ie quality or budget.

[Changing ways of working shouldn't comprise merely of adding things to do. Remove at least as many.]

I wonder if in a parallel universe where the USSR had continued to exist, with the Cold War rivalry continuing to spew technical wonders like moon landings and Concorde... would we have cracked exothermic nuclear fusion? Competition for progress is a miraculous force.

A choice between two options contains a hidden third: not choosing. Whether that's good or bad depends on the reasons for having the options.

Things that are exceptionally fast tend to also be exceptionally fragile. And exceptionally far off mark when aimed incorrectly or stopped too late."

The luckier people are, the more they'll believe it's their god-given talent.

"The market's just not ready for this yet." – Nice excuse for when you get it completely wrong.

Can we have a moment on the effect that "Highly Effective People" have on everyone else? They pretty f'ing annoying to be around.

Monitoring. Don't confuse "concern for the monitored" with "paranoia of the monitorer". Even if embedded in one and the same person.

[**A: "There is no 'I' in 'Team'."**
B: "There is no 'I' in 'Blame' either."
A: "Hahaha LOL. FU."]

Hey MBA, believe it or not, but some things don't need managing. Same for some people.

"Just pick up the f-ing phone" – what Outlook should advise you whenever you start typing yet another reply-email.

Compromise: when you can't agree.

Hey leader, are you in front of your troops or on the hill in the back?

Asking more people more questions feels like you're getting closer to a truth, until more answers start conflicting. Which IS the truth.

[WD40] = or ≠ [Repair]. Discuss.

[Customer Centricity score] = [External email volume] / [Internal email volume].

No one ever risk-reduced their way to growth.

To convince a committee, befriend the WHOLE committee. Because the purpose of a committee is that no members can/want/dare choose alone.

[If the time won by delegating a task cannot be used to create additional value, then you shouldn't have delegated.]

I don't think you need a fax number on your business card anymore.

It's better having a stupid system with smart people, than a smart system with stupid people. The former adapts, the latter crumbles

Realizing at the end of a phone conference, having given smart nuggets all the way to steer conversation, that you were on mute throughout.

'Micro-managing' is in the eye of the beholder.

"Gen-Y are so agile in their decision making!" – Because they're still young and their responsibilities are a fraction of the older Gen's.

Why entrepreneurs work day & night? Coz they aren't driven by the small odds of making a fortune, but by the big odds of losing a fortune.

Hey barista, I think I'm old enough to carry my coffee to the condiments counter without a lid. Trust me on this one.

THE CIRCULAR ECONOMY BETTER HAVE SOME PATH-DEPENDANT DIRECTIONALITY, OR I'M OUT.

Planning hysteresis.
It's endlessly easier to overrun than to underrun. But that's typically not built into plans.

The only (and truly only) situation you need a perfect start, is when you won't be able to course correct. And that's almost never the case.

Risk: you can form an opinion about it, but you can't measure it. Unless it's not your own risk, then measuring is easy.

"First time right" only matters if you can make it on time too.

What do you call the opposite of "the gift that keeps on giving"?

Benefits & Risks do not sit in the same dimensions, as some kind of zero sum, balanced act. Both should be weighed and treated separately.

You cannot disrupt a market without disrupting your own organization.

Measures to reduce Risk will also reduce Luck, as the unexpected can't be classified before it presents itself.

My new concept timeline: "Preferably Yesterday", "ASAP" and "Narnia".

Planning a business war-game? Look up on LinkedIn the actual people in key roles at your competitors. More personal & insightful than SWOTs.

Being overly positive or negative about a process is quite pointless if you haven't yet agreed a destination, or even a direction.

Popular press gets excited about "Life Possible On Proximus Centauri B", skipping the fact we haven't even (dis)proven life on Mars yet.

You can have excellent overview from close by.
It's just an overview of fewer, smaller things.

The word 'Innovation' is mostly used to describe with hindsight what someone has already done, and done successfully enough to get noticed.

Opportunities come and go? Nonsense. Missed opportunities will haunt you forever.

Strategic U-turns, aka pivots... Don't just bounce from left to right and black to white without considering the middle. Lots of greys in between.

TQM Equivalent of a Gordian knot: try explaining heuristics to a Six Sigma Black Belt. To get moving, you just cut the Black Belt in half.

Preparing for a sales meeting? All you need to bring are one or two good metaphors. Seriously, that's all you need.

Pass stuff up to the echelon of decision makers & they'll do exactly that: make a decision. So pass up only when you are sure a decision is needed.

Hey entrepreneur: hire people so good you that would fire yourself if you had been in their role.

Every day is groundcoffee day.

Too few corporate hotshots have a section on their CV that records "things I made".

Straight to the periphery of the problem.

Feeling your back against the wall? An illusion because the wall is probably moving your way and pushing you.

Flying out of Brazil, CWB Gate 2. That place that mysteriously always smells of cheese.

Are you receiving challenges, or creating them?

Are your customer acquisition manager and customer retention manager still working from separate offices?

Urgent? How urgent? "Annoyed-urgent", "Sweating-urgent" or "Peeing-in-pants-urgent"?

"OMG It's *sooo* busy and we are so behind on schedule!! Let's discuss what to do after we get back from holiday in 6 weeks" – Your colleagues.

Detail-focused or detail-distracted?

Personal growth feeds business growth and vice versa. But business contraction also feeds personal growth.

Business empires crumble from risk-aversity, losing their willingness to embrace change. Make that any empire.

"As Seen On TV!" – remember that was considered a good enough reason to buy?

Real innovation requires changing the angle of decision making from "stop unless" into "let pass unless", as you have no clear benchmark.

Distract the naysayers with red herrings like neuro-MR and big data, while you get the real work done.

I THINK MY HAMBURG HOTEL ELEVATOR IS WARNING ME ABOUT TAXI APP STOCK.

Right now, a colleague of yours is thinking of all the things you should do better too.

Are you paddling or sailing?

New in the #superhero line-up: The Incredible Innovation Man... jumps to conclusions faster than a speeding bullet.

The title slide of your presentation says more than a thousand words. So, skip the thousand words and move to slide 2, please.

[**Most of what you lack in influence, you can make up with persuasion. And vice versa.**]

Better to include 50% extra time for mistakes and start immediately, than wasting 50% extra time planning up front and presume no mistakes.

Ideas put on +2 year horizon "for technical reasons" are only that far out for lack of willpower. Almost anything is technically possible within 2 years.

[**Think twice, and then again, before telling someone they don't know what they're doing.**]

Beware of the planner who promises running at optimal capacity.

Translating every decision into a financial one is merely a mental trick to help you feel morally exempt from the effects of that decision.

Ask yourself – what's the best metaphor to describe my job?

When gambling, gamble some chickens and maybe a goat. Never the whole ranch and certainly not your spouse. #Metaphor

"We need more examples" – always, regardless of how many examples you provide.

French in-flight announcements in English are the audio equivalent of a doctor's scribble on a prescription. Important but incomprehensible.

Long ago, people thought you'd fall off At World's End. I still think that at AMS H7.

"Wait a minute... maybe I'M the problem myself!?" – only enlightened people.

[**Courage: put your intuition out in the open for scrutiny, ahead of the facts coming in.**]

Risk averse mind-set: delusion all options can be known before starting. Innovation success originates in one's confidence to course correct.

"10 Tips to harness your business growth" – As if today's businesses need constraints on their unsustainable, life-threatening growth.

"The first thing we're doing to get out of this mess my predecessor left, is create a new logo." – New CEO's.

The fundamental difference between fast/cheap innovation programmes and long/expensive ones is the amount of risk/ambiguity one's accepting.

"No Action" is often the better option, but less understood by stakeholders and impossible to take credit for.

What you struggle to understand, trying to explain it will just take you further away. Let your subconscious play with it for a few days.

CPG/FMCG Innovation teams tend to overlook there's really only one party they need to convince: the retailer selling their stuff.

You can't instruct someone to be more entrepreneurial. At best, you can remove restraints that weren't self-imposed.

Be brave and work towards an ambitious new comfort zone.
'Design Thinking' anagrams to 'Thin Skinned Gig'

Suggested names for the ratio between 'energy spent debating an idea' versus 'energy it would take to pilot the idea' on a spectrum from 0<1 & 1<∞.
- The Inertia Threshold
- The Tinkerer's Razor
- The Inventor's Facepalm
- Chatterbox over Sandbox score
- Tittle-tattle to go-to-battle index
- Elbowing to elbow grease
- Slagging over slogging gap
- The Worrier/Warrior Scale

Failure, Defeat and Ruin – three very different things, but often raked onto one pile by risk analysts and inspirational quote writers.

I ran GVA Security to D75 in under four minutes. I'm sure that's worth some kind of formal accreditation?

Work experience stages
1) I want to join the machine
2) Help I'm a cog in the machine
3) Fight the machine
4) OMG There is no machine

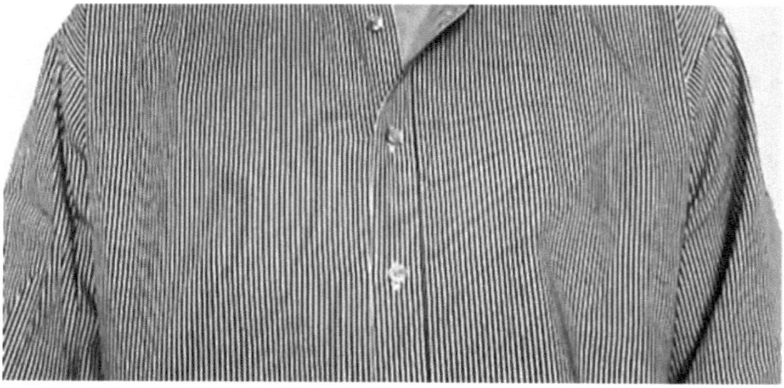

PRO-TIP FOR VIDEO CONFERENCING PRANKS: WEAR A MOIRÉ-EFFECT INDUCING STRIPED SHIRT TO ANNOY EVERYONE INSTANTLY.

Disruptive Start-ups are a little bit like tempestuous teenagers, they need to go out and try their wild stuff... and find for themselves that not all of the old ways were bad. Progress is about breaking ties with the past selectively, rather than totally.

[Excuses for unprofitable activity]
"We always do it this way!"
"It's strategic!"
"The other thing was even worse!"
"Need to do SOMEthing!"

When embarking on an journey, "I got your back" is worth infinitely more than "Good luck"

Occam's Razor redux: never attribute to talent what can adequately be described as luck.

Can one have multiple Comfort Zones?

'BE QUIET, DON'T EVEN BREATHE' What I think while I struggle to find the 'disconnect' button after the goodbyes at the end of a conference call.

Every product category has a metaphorical equivalent to 'weeds'.

Open Innovation is difficult, because large companies are set up to buy raw materials, services and other companies. Not for buying ideas.

I wonder if Apple Inc would have been as successful if the Steves had given it a modern day, misspelled, stupid name like Appl, APPEL, Aqqle, ... ?!

I suspect the majority of feuds between Marketing and R&D teams originated when one team said “feasible” and the other heard “affordable”.

I've only seen a fraction of the poorly used iceberg metaphors in business presentations.

Pro travel tip: when without travel adapter, use the USB port on the back of your hotel room TV to charge your phone

'We need to communicate better' is often actioned as 'We need to send more emails'

Many organizations understand the importance of systematic removal of cost but forget the equivalent importance of systematic addition of value.

Short business books should be more expensive than long ones. If they're written from experience, that is.

"Glacial" is a speed.
And “backwards” is a direction.
LOOK AT THE BRIGHT SIDE OF THINGS

Ensure to take care not to double up on additional pleonasms in your PowerPoint presentation slides.

I suspect a good way to break into a building is to come dressed as an alarm maintenance person.

[The anvil is in the detail.]

'Am I willing to work through weekends to make this thing work?' #ForgottenInnovationQuestions

An exceptionally safe place to store passwords nowadays, is a 5.25" floppy disk. Guaranteed unreadable except by the most expert of experts.

Skunkwork projects running 'below radar' in your business reveal the remarkable truth that in reality, difficulties come from within rather than outside.

Maybe we just blockchain some of these blockchain experts, for some peace & quiet?

Excellence is a moving target – everywhere except in ISO process manuals.

It strikes me as quite desperate how non-US retailers across the globe have copied 'Black Friday Sales' after a perfectly normal Thursday.

What makes you more "tourist"?
1) Repacking your luggage at check-in counter.
2) Debating 300ml shampoo bottle with scanner operator

Kodak, Nokia, Polaroid – Juicy stories where large companies lost out to changing times. BUT they are anomalies. The big players almost always win.

Every time you say Millennial, a Baby Boomer dies.
[Paraphrasing Mr Rikki Marr]

Let's be honest. 50 years of pushing the food pyramid as healthy diet has left half the global population with love handles. Often significant, flabby love handles.

[Discomfort strengthens.]

“I'm SO busy!” – worst last words.

I see on TikTok that Gen-Z has discovered the fun of Mentos® & Coke®.

Post-its don't kill workshops. Pointless creative exercises kill workshops.

Maybe you could 3D print yourself out of trouble?

Don't see everything you believe.

You don't want a cheap tattoo. Or a hasty doctor. Carry that mentality across into other parts of your life, it'll be better for it.

Disruptive innovation requires disruptive people. Aka the kind that corporate environments tend to neutralize with KPI's.

Bought a Fitbit. Now considering cheats.

If you're regularly out of stock – do you have a distribution problem, or a pricing problem?

Is it me, or are dual presentations on conference stages (as in, two people together) almost always confusing? It's seldom done for the benefit of the audience.

Not seen any over-excited tweets about Hyperloop in my feed for a while. Anyone still working on that?

Free upgrades to business class still make me squeal like a teenage tourist.

'Disruptive Innovation' anagrams to
- 'Avid Intuitions, Proven'
- 'Intuitive Non-Pro Divas'
- 'Purist, Avoid Invention'"

'Launch' isn't a moment or phase transition, but a period of time. Quite a long one actually.

The worst thing you can do to an insecure decision maker: feed them even more good alternatives.

"Roughly right" beats "Precisely wrong", always.

It's probably wise to scrap all ambitions for disruptive innovation if your procurement team can't register new suppliers in less than 6 months.

Hotel alarm clocks: the least trusted devices on earth.

Every success story I know involves some degree of plain luck. Therefor do keep some of your work unplanned, simply to stumble on something good you hadn't expected.

“He has visionary ideas, just not very realistic" – in other words, quite useless.

If you're not the type to procrastinate, you can choose to over-intellectualize instead.

MS Project – meant for planning projects but instead used for recording what actually happened.

[Looks at clock for mercy]
[None granted, as usual]

Hey retailers, I'm pretty sure Monday can't count as Black Friday anymore. Hold yourself together please.

'B' and 'E' – the inflight seating equivalent of drawing the short straw.

Interpreting Parkinson's Law. Don't complain about the pointless reporting you do, unless you can show what you'd rather do with time instead.

Your faith in statistical confidence correlates directly with the amount of your own money sunk in the implications of acting upon it.

Happy-anger, aka WTF-anger, can be a very powerful and positive creative force.

The value is remembered long after the price is forgotten.

Risk is less perceived in context of potential reward, and more in perspective of potential ruin.

Epilogue: When The World Falls Apart

I'LL PASS THIS PROJECT ON TO
YOUR SUCCESSOR, NEXT YEAR OR SO.
CAN YOU CREATE A HANDOVER DECK?
BTW YOU KNOW YOU'RE FIRED, RIGHT?

Epilogue: When The World Falls Apart

I'm compiling this 3rd Grumpy Innovator book three months into the 2020 Corona crisis and a market meltdown. That's pretty tough if you're running a small business. And the outlook is worrying, to say the least. What now? If you're reading this after everything has returned to prosperity, well done on surviving! If the pandemic is still raging, read on.

For what it's worth, a few thoughts for owners and entrepreneurs of small businesses, especially the young ones. At Happen we were just over a year old when we went through a similar global economic collapse in 2008 when Lehman Brothers fell.

Daily business seemed to evaporate overnight. Everything changed, just like it 2020 is proving to do. Back then, we survived and eventually thrived. Plenty of luck and good business friends obviously, but what else?

First and foremost: **be aware you have control**. As a small, self-owned business, you can respond much quicker (and in your own favour) better than you ever could as a large business. That said, if you're over your eyeballs in VC then it's someone else's money at stake and you might as well walk away now. Screw 'em and start over. Or make an offer to buy back your business for peanuts, in full. You know your business better than they do.

Throw your old business plan out the window, if you even had one to start with. Its assumptions will prove mostly nostalgic, even laughable a few years from now.

The paranoid survive. By that I do not mean that taking risks or changing track is bad, on the contrary. But you can only go bust once and the threshold for going bust will now be much lower.

The market will get much worse before it gets better because second-order effects still need to kick in. In fact this time it is worse to start with, given Corona prevents people interacting normally outside of the financial markets. Things will not return to the old state, the new normal will be different when it settles down 2-3 years from now. Which might be a longer waiting period than you've even been in business for.

Your client portfolio will need to change quickly, as all of them will be going through frantic change themselves now. Your current largest client might disappear, a tiny one might become huge. As long as you're willing to change quickly yourself.

Business development before delivery. This should actually always be the case if you intend to grow, but it's even more true now. Do you have a team who can convince clients to continue to work with you? Are they just mouths to feed, or are they feeding you back? Take a hard, honest look.

Immerse in the debt situation of your clients, and the fragility of the industry they are in. Then be brutal in your choice which ones to stay away from, or ask up-front payment from. Your pockets probably aren't very deep. So your time and resource is better spent on finding new clients that represent the new normal, than potentially losing everything on a fragile client taking your revenue down with them.

Adapt your offer to what matters in the new world, to keep your clients' projects moving. Prevent stalling, your clients will love you for being nimble. For us, the main new innovation methodologies we developed in those days were

'Sweating Assets', i.e. innovate asset-out from the factory to guarantee 'zero CapEx required' for your innovation. Also, it triggered us to develop online research tools (radical in 2008) which led to the birth of our Winkle team in 2009; now Happen Research & Analytics.

Cash is King... hold on to it, EVERY PENNY. Spread it across multiple banks, as even banks can topple. Any expense not serving your primary purpose is an expense wasted. Also "Leaders eat last", as per ancient adagium. Your own salary can wait, as that's also cost to the business: one that you can choose to raise again in better times.

Know your 'uncle point' and act on it. Instead of trying to predict how things will unfold (no one can) make 100% clear to yourself what your worst acceptable situation is, the rock-bottom at which you pull the kill switch. This might be ahead of a next round of monthly payments. This is important because entrepreneurial optimism might drag you deeper into trouble than you can afford.

Pay your suppliers on time, all of them. As a small business, your survival might be dependent on them as much as vice versa. Also, you probably know them personally, and they know your business and category deeply. They are the best sounding board for evolving your business into the new reality.

Prepare for longer payment terms to become standard. Back in 2008, most of our clients went up from 30 to 60 or even 90 days and have stayed there since. I wouldn't be surprised to see that go up to 90 and 120 across the board. Organize your business to be able to deal with this and keep the clients who do pay faster close to your heart with extra service. Equally, be merciless in chasing outstanding invoices. Hiring someone to chase them for you will free you up to hunt new business.

Remember that as owner you are in control and surrounded by entrepreneurial employees who enjoy the hustle of being in a small business. A team who will be more willing to change track and try new things with you than you might think!

In the meantime, stay safe and prosper.

Democracy is on a slippery slope when/where people approach it as a consumer right rather than a civilian duty.

[Entropy always wins. Life is literally about fighting it to the death.]

Dutch proverb: "If you burn your ass, you must sit on the blisters". Relevant stuff, those Dutch proverbs.

An MBA might get your career unstuck, but not your life. You need other things for that.

"Shaken, not stirred" – James Bond describing how his first project debrief made him feel.

Reality = Actual facts
Observation = Perceived facts
Story = Interpreted facts
BS = Created facts
Profile = Selective facts
Evidence = Any"

When looking back at hectic periods of your life, ask not HOW you coped, but WHY you coped. Much more interesting.

Is the system corrupted or has the corruption become systematic?

Did you know "Professional Lobbyist" anagrams to "Booby Trap Of Silliness".

To all politicians. Before opening your mouth, ask yourself "Would my mother approve of what I'm about to say?". Thank you.

We preach to the converted because it's easier.

Contrary to popular belief, a vegan diet of muesli burgers, organic carrot cake, soy Frappuccino® & organic beer still makes you fat.

Hypothesis: Western societal cohesion began fragmenting & drifting apart when military service was ended mid 90's and adolescents mixed less.

Fraud types:
A: Nincompoop who tumbles into it and can't stop.
B: Ruthless, manipulating opportunist.
Note: A is an illusion created by B.

"I don't get it. My presentation is clear, concise, I even do a bit of theatre. BUT NO ONE EVEN LOOKS UP." – Air hostess safety instruction.

We call it 'GMO' because 'selective inbreeding' doesn't sound nice, right?

Yes clickbait, we get it now.

When you realize that you still have over half a bag of disgusting coffee beans to grind through before you can switch back to a brand you like.

When the only power socket at the whole airport is next to the toilets' entrance. Feeling like a real junkie.

[Why fool others when it's so much easier just to fool yourself?]

A: "Is it walking distance?"
B: "About 20 minutes."
A: "So no."
Why humanity will not live to be 100.

Hey startup, work/think in earn-rates, not burn-rates. Seriously.

Cynics say the world runs on PowerPoint. But we all know that isn't true. It runs on Excel.

Isn't it ironic how businesses big enough to have a 'scenario planning team' are too big to adapt in time for any of their scenarios?

Anyone complaining that technocrats are running government too much like a business is giving too much credit to how most businesses are run

I don't know anyone who got fired for trying something new. But know a couple struggling to get hired for never having tried.

Sadly, many people consider their body no more than a vessel that carries their head around from A to B. Or worse, only their eyes & mouth.

I saw a DeLorean drive through The Hague this evening, which must be a happy omen of some kind.

"Live like there's no tomorrow!"
aka "Hopelessly stuck in yesterday."

Be patient, time flies anyway.

Fundamentalists and Atheists both never give serendipity the credit it deserves, mistaking it either for divine intervention or skill.

"Wow, someone actually bought something." – Air hostess after a duty-free round through the aisle, when someone actually bought something.

"Haha LOL, look at Greece struggling with their debt of 2x GDP" – Says person with a mortgage 6x their annual income.

Is the love-hate relationship politicians have with their voters comparable to marketers and their consumers? Just a hunch.

It's easier to care than to pretend to care.

The Titanic: everyone was so preoccupied with the lack of lifeboats, no one considered the iceberg as a fine place to wait for a few hours.

Merci bacon, Auto-correcte.

"And don't make any mistakes, OK?" – Useless advice given 1000's of times every day.

Access = Power

Dutch proverb: "When you're being shaven, sit very still". Relevant stuff, those Dutch proverbs.

Pre-industrial ages: Stone, Bronze & Iron.
Post-industrial ages: Stoned, Bronzed and Ironed.

Clearly demonstrated by the VW Diesel Swindle is what happens when regulators know less of the topic than the regulated. Think IT, Pharma...

Who cares about late departures? It's late arrivals that are the annoyance.

The Herd works in mysterious ways.

When you're desperate for good news, n=1 is suddenly good enough.

Western democracy went kaputt when politicians started acting as marketers to consumers of civil services – and citizens acted accordingly.

"Passengers with small children board first" – which doesn't apply to "Passengers squealing like small children".

Inserting more energy into a system, be it human/machine/environment doesn't increase its power, but its volatility.

Doing in-flight yoga poses in your airplane seat makes you look like a jerk. Or whatever the feminine word for of jerk is.

The current era of central banking policies will be known as "The Homeopathy Decade", when infinitely small rates were thought to heal.

Millennials say "Whoop!" too often.

"If you don't like our train service, then go take a train somewhere else."
– Service logic of train companies.

My worry isn't about more robots becoming smarter than humans. My worry is about more humans becoming dumber than robots.

When you suspect the system is corrupted, corruption probably is the system.

Politicians zoom in on the differences, diplomats on the commonalities. Which is why politicians should stay away from negotiations.

To all you nitpickers out there: have a ncie weeknd!

If the Internet were a country, it would be a pretty horrible place to live. A surveillance state full of thieves and con artists. Oh wait.

Landed at London Luton airport, which isn't in London. On to Luton Parkway station, in a bus. And the station isn't in Luton either.
This place is a web of lies.

[I bet that of every $1 generated by digital start-ups, $3 is spent on hyping the stock.]

Trade shrinks the differences between two countries, Politics increases them. Trade builds bridges, Politics burn them.

Evaluating my Generation-X heritage...
Ambition: Fight Club
Reality: Jackass
Legacy: Gluten-free

Trade accelerates mutual interests, interdependencies and personal conversation between people who would otherwise be strangers.

The world would be a much better place if we all took more naps. Proper, middle-of-the-day siestas.

When it comes to stimulating trade, governments can only place or remove restrictions. Via Negativa.

After 12 years of frequent flying, the one thing I've still not perfected is my disembark-to-bus technique. I always end at Customs last.

Sadly, being more opinionated is too often interpreted as being better informed.

Don't moan about today's price of cigarettes if you're happy to spend $5 on a single latte.

The quality of institutions isn't defined by the quality of their leader, but by its resilience to unqualified idiots leading it off course.

If airlines truly understood frequent flyers, the reward tiers wouldn't be Bronze-Silver-Gold but OMG-MEH-FML.

[You can recognize a first world economy by the amount of money spent on fighting boredom.]

History: a long string of events that prove people wrong, who thought they were right at the time.

Empathy: acceptance the other side simply doesn't know they're wrong yet.

Friday afternoon, an easyJet flight from Luton to Amsterdam. Smells of anticipation, shored up by cheap deodorant.

A: "Describe yourself in one word."
B: "Mildly rebellious."

Rank the quality of any country's institutions by whether the move people, or money upwards through the system.

In the grand scheme of things, 'grand' is probably giving today's schemes too much credit.

Antiquity. More or less the same as today, but without the penicillin, electricity and plastic.

So far, I find Brexit an anticlimax of Y2K proportions.

Business traveler truth: all beaten-up 767's end up servicing routes to Heathrow.

When will the homeopaths weigh in on #COVID19? You'd think this is their moment to shine, no?

I doubt I will recognize any April Fools' pranks today as being jokes.

Obviously once the lockdown is lifted, we'll see a dramatic rise in divorces filed ... with the dark twist that now both parties will ask for the other partner to keep the damn kids.

Right now would be a good time to prove existence of life on another planet, to put today's agitations in some well-needed perspective.

Reviving a 100 million year old microbe isnt very different from fast-forwarding the genetic code by 100 million years, aka GMO. The organism and environment haven't evolved in parallel.

Paraphrasing a friend of mine, long ago: "If you can make it to 50 without 'growing up' then your environment will absolve you of that expectation". I was too young at the time to understand that was a good thing.

Anyone complaining that members of the European Parliament lead too lavish lifestyles should come check out Strasbourg Airport. What a dump.

Shock a woke Millennial by explaining people in wheelchairs can be assholes too.

Watching 'Die Hard 2', appalled by 1990's lack of airport security.

As humans, we're horrible at distinguishing permanent versus temporary, and vice versa.

Airports without power plugs deserve to have their vending machines unplugged so I can charge my phone. I'm talking to you, Milan Linate.

[The virtue of "tolerance" is mostly a well disguised "indifference", which isn't very virtuous at all.]

Broadsheet news headlines containing the words "could", "might" and "expected to" are mostly not much better than fake news and buzzfeeds.

Only in New York... it's half past seven in the morning and I've already spent $12 on coffee.

Is it me, or is the Moral High Ground getting really crowded?

Big ideas can pull people, communities or even a whole nation together. Or drive them apart.

If an alien landed, commanding 'Take Me To Your Leader' ... you can imagine the confusion that would give nowadays.

**JULY 4TH IS THE ANNIVERSARY OF THE PASSING OF THESE TWO LOVELY HUMANS.
BE LIKE BOB. BE LIKE BARRY.
THE WORLD WILL BE A LITTLE BETTER FOR IT.**

If your public persona is slick & polished, the only way to gain street cred seems to be a complete public unravelling, breakdown, followed by a miraculous upswing.

Nothing says 'Monday Morning' like a Citrix logon experience.

After Boomers, GenX, Millennials and GenZ, 2021 will give us The Coronials. Born out of bored parents working from home for a couple of months.

From personal experience in 2008. Big & small businesses will indeed implode in coming months. And then LOTS of new small businesses will be created in next 1-2 years, some of which grow into the next generation of big ones.

It's much easier to form an objective opinion when you're not fully informed. The more info, the more subjective is your interpretation.

Airport perfume counters have become dystopian IKEA labyrinths. I'm talking to you, Gatwick Airport South Terminal.

Paraphrasing what I remember someone saying in the early 2000's about the fall of the Soviet Union: "Bookstores used to sell only Politburo-approved literature and Solzhenitsyn would be impossible to find. Now bookstores can sell anything they want, but only stock Stephen King."

"But my camera is on?!" – poor guy in a Zoom call who happens to have a very round face and eyes that look like his initials.

Young people who are still yapping "Covid won't kill you if you're under 60" clearly haven't thought through what "almost dying" implies.

At current innovation ambition levels, we'll end this century as we did the last one, just with Facebook and worse weather. PROGRESS PLEASE.

Baby Boomers are the first human generation to grow into adulthood without siblings dying young, thanks to penicillin. Many of them felt immortal, trusting medicine with carry them into old age. Then #COVID19 knocked on their door, to settle old debts from a life lived poorly.

What economists call growth is like saying "I jumped up in the air" without adding "and into a manhole"

I think there's a correlation between the flight seat row where the Business/Economy split screen is pegged, and the Dow Jones index.

I believe charities should have an explicit, statutory purpose of making themselves obsolete after resolving the problem they were created for.

The spectrum of life in COVID lockdown;
Elderly: life as usual
Couples with no kids: life's good
Couples with young kids: kill me
Couples with older kids: this ain't a hotel dammit
Singles: OMG booooored f**k this celibacy

If your ego drives you to calling yourself 'CEO' of small start-up, then I think 'Secretary General' is more appropriate.

What have you taken for granted recently?

I guess the Burglary industry is now switching from Consumer to Professional, with the lockdown making their work in our homes impossible.

OMG I am now 4 years older than Danny Glover was in the first Lethal Weapon went he kept saying he was too old for this shit.

I remember simpler days, when it was just Rage Against The Answering Machine.

Kind of funny to be reminded that The Kilogram is an agreement, not a thing.

Across the world, parents now working from home are having to explain their kids "yes this is what I do all day".

Your revenues might be down in these daunting times, but imagine the world emerging from lockdown and finding that nobody missed your products? Seek being relevant to your customers before anything else.

Working from home I get a lot done, but I sit so still my Fitbit thinks I died.

I love how breweries and distilleries are making sanitizer gels and giving them away for free. To keep the good vibes flowing, I have asked some of our clients who make sanitizers to switch to beer and spirits and give them away for free too.

I guess 'anti-fragility' is life's way of dealing with 'entropy' and coming out on top.

Sadly, very [narrow + polarized] messages are parading as clarity.

One full lap completed. By 'lap' I mean a full orbit around the Sun.

Gents, taking phone calls while standing at a urinal is just wrong – on so many levels.

I'M NOT FEELING ANY PURPOSE ALIGNED WITH OUR ESSENCE HERE. CAN YOU PRETOTYPE A FEW MORE MVP'S FOR CO-CREATION?

Glossary of Innovation ~~Bullshit Bingo~~ terms

Normal People	Innovation People
3Y Plan θri:yɪər plæn – noun A plan covering the next three calendar years. *We bought the royal mansion and made a 3Y plan for restoring it to its former glory.*	A 1Y plan, made to celebrate highlights from the past year and project them onto the next. Re-written every year from scratch, to align objectives to new bonus targets. *I was challenged on my 3Y plan not delivering the desired growth, so I upped Y2 and Y3 for my successor.*
360° View θri:sɪkstivju: - noun A 'full circle' approach or view into a situation. *We enjoyed a 360° view of our surroundings, and could see for miles and miles into the distance.*	Tends to imply an approach involving 2 to 10 parties, with the objective, perspective and outcomes optimised to the person sitting at the centre of that 360-degree panorama. *For [product] to make any profit, we'll need a 360 approach to saving cost.* *Designer vantage: squeeze R&D, Manufacturing and Procurement* *Procurement vantage: squeeze Manufacturing, Suppliers, expedition*
2025 Vision twɛn ti twɛn ti faɪvˈvɪʒ ən – noun A view on the year 2025. *We imagine buying a house in 2025.*	A chance to re-state all ambitions originally set for 2020 but trashed by the Covid crisis and naive forecasting. Given it's comfortably 4½ years out, also a chance to up the game a bit. *The cupholder brand's CMO pictured a 2025 vision of a hot beverage on the handlebars of every self-steering motorbike in the world. Bold!*
Accelerator əkˈsɛləreɪtɔr - noun Lever connected to energy source in vehicle drive train. For example, the right foot pedal in car. *Stamping hard on the accelerator is referred to as "Pedal To The Metal".*	An organisation that provides small amounts of cash, coaching and office space to a large number of start-ups named after popular nouns but with missing vowels. A numbers game, the objective being to get some of them to survive past a second investment round, so the shares can be sold on to the next sucker at profit. *The Accelerator housed 25 start-ups, 24 of which failed. But the sale of their stock in "Bleedr" made them enough return to fund another 50.*

Normal People	Innovation People
Adjacency əˈdʒeɪ sən si - noun An area right next to where you are. *Pete stood next to me, making him an adjacency to me.*	A product, occasion or opportunity that is just outside one's typical playing field. The benefit of working on finding a good adjacency is the potential to leverage technology and other business assets in a 'Blue Ocean' of opportunity, not having to build it from scratch. Comes with the bonus of a fresh set of competitors. *Dentures for cats.* *Spotify for 40+ year olds.* *Chocolate for men.*
Agile adʒʌɪl - adjective Able to move quickly and easily. *Ruth hopped from queue to queue, agile as a little monkey.*	A development and project planning methodology drawn from software development, transplanted to every other category under the sun. Often misunderstood because it has such a nice name. *Assemble a scrum team and get to work. See you next week, I want the outputs of sprint 1 on my desk at 08h30, thanks.*
Alignment əˈlʌɪnm(ə)nt - noun Arrangement in a straight line or in correct relative positions. *The tiles had slipped out of alignment.*	To agree something amongst a number of stakeholders. Often mistaken for talking about project status and filling the Outlook slot. *Can we align where you got to with that brief? Please ping me a Teams invite.*
Archetypes ɑːkɪtʌɪp - noun A very typical example of a certain person or thing. *He was the archetype of the old-skool advertising man.*	Simplification of consumer behaviour in the form of cliché personalities, aka personas. Often trademarked by research agencies and re-skinned for different clients and given stupid names. *"It was only when I moved to from Dairy to Detergents, that I realised Helga The Hunter-Gatherer and Elsa The Optimist Extravert were the same persona"*

Normal People	Innovation People
Asset-Out asɛt'aʊt - adjective Methodology that implies working within the constraints of existing assets, mostly referring to manufacturing lines. Not to be mistaken with 'Assed-Out'. *These pet snacks were developed asset-out from the pet food lines, saving a lot of time and CapEx.*	This is how every small business innovates, which is to start from existing capabilities. In larger organisations, where innovation teams, R&D, marketing and manufacturing might all sit in different countries or even continents, it's easy to lose sight of what is actually feasible and pragmatic. *When there's no money left to invest in new factory lines, make something asset-out on the old lines to keep going.*
Augmented Reality ɔːɡˈmɛntɪd'rɪˈalɪtl - noun A technology that superimposes a computer-generated image on a user's view of the real world, thus providing a composite view. *Every tech company under the sun is trying to find a sensible purpose for Augmented Reality.*	A persistent belief that everything one can peer at through a camera lens will become a magical experience by layering additional information on top. Very few examples outside of professional applications have proven viable, or technically stable enough to last. *Point your phone's camera at café in front of you and read information provided that it's a café.*
Axplore ækˈsplɔr- verb No equivalent in regular human language	Formally known as 'blamestorming', but more action oriented. Travel through an (unfamiliar) area in order to find out who's fault it is. *"He axplored the team & fired Henry"*
Behavioral Change bɪˈheɪvjər(ə)l'tʃeɪn(d)ʒ - noun A change of routine, usually after an intervention or dramatic event. *The mere sight of the cattle prod is enough to elicit behaviour change from even the most stubborn of toddlers.*	Usually refers to habit change rather than behaviour change. A prime purpose in life for many marketers is to claim they have 'achieved a behaviour change' amongst their brand's consumers by switching them to a new habit that involves increased consumption of their product. *Dentures for cats.* *Spotify for 40+ year olds.* *Chocolate for men.*

Normal People	Innovation People
Blue Ocean bluˈoʊ ʃən - noun Definition of a market opportunity, based on disrupting a market adjacent to one's own. Usually a market that can be simplified and democratized. Read the book by INSEAD professors W. Chan Kim and Renée Mauborgn. *Stelios spotted the Blue Ocean of no-frills air travel, founded easyJet® and gave British Airways lots of pain.*	A product, occasion or opportunity that is just outside one's typical playing field. The benefit of working on finding a good Blue Ocean is the potential to leverage technology and other business assets on an adjacent opportunity, not having to build it from scratch. Comes with the bonus of a fresh set of competitors. *Our ocean is turning too Red for comfort. Find me a nice and empty Blue one please.*
Big Data bɪgˈdeɪtə - noun Extremely large datasets that may be analysed computationally to reveal patterns, trends, and associations, especially relating to human behaviour. *Much IT investment is being done in acquiring, managing and maintaining Big Data.*	In an increasingly digital world, data is being generated by almost every human interaction imaginable. This data is collected in 'lakes' for analysis and spotting useful patterns. *"I NEED MOAR DATA"*
Burn Rate bəːn reɪt - noun The speed at which a fire, flame or glow consumes a fuel such as coal or wood. *A fire burned and crackled cheerfully in the grate, we knew we'd be comfortable for the evening.*	Speed at which an organisation is spending its investors' money. Not to be confused with entrepreneurship, which involves spending one's own money. *They're buying companies like they're swiping through f-ing Tinder®. At this burn rate they'll be dead by Xmas.*

Normal People	Innovation People
Burning platform ˈbɜr nɪŋ ˈplæt fɔrm - noun A raised construction that has been set alight. *The Brighton Pier for a few hours in May 2003.*	A topic of paramount importance to the business, or at least the CEO, for the survival of the business. *Snack food CEO's have made "healthy snacking" a burning platform, to keep regulators from intervening.*
Cat man kæt mæn - noun Male cartoon character of mixed human/feline form. *Batman's nemesis Cat Man struck again.*	Category Manager, carrying responsibility over a defined part of the product/service portfolio of an organisation. Often referring to a subset that has no equivalent outside of the organisation amongst customers or consumers. *Since my promotion to Cat Man,* *I look after our P&L for Juicy Crackers.*
Circular Economy ˈsɜr kyə lər ɪˈkɒn ə mi - noun A closed economy of goods, with no depletion of (natural) resources. *We sort and recycle different plastic waste products to convert into virgin material for the packaging industry.*	A particular spin on Sustainability principles, that drives for closed circle (flow) of materials. Waste is minimised and after the usable life of a product, its materials and components are reused for a new product. *Greta told the world leaders at Davos to go circular or go home.*
Co-creation kokriːˈeɪʃ(ə)n - noun The action or process of bringing something into existence, together with someone else *creation of a coalition government*	Ideation with consumers, or by consumers while you watch from behind a 1-way mirror. *Our R&D team has run out of ideas, so we're opting to co-create some with some random people we plucked from the street.*

Normal People	Innovation People
Consumer Centric kən'su mər 'sɛn trɪk - adjective When your business decision-making revolves around (pleasing) your consumer base. *In an age of concern about pleasing shareholders over source of business, 'Consumer Centricity' has become a virtue signal.*	Many businesses express consumer centricity by taking every decision to focus groups. This is analogous to asking what your friend wants for their birthday, then giving that, and being disappointed they're not happily surprised. *When the snacking brand team asked consumers if they preferred more or less chocolate, they said 'MORE' and now the business case won't close.*
Cradle 2 Cradle 'kreɪd(ə)l'tʊ''kreɪd(ə)l - noun Moving from one baby's bed (or co) to the next. *The desperate, first-time parents moved the crying baby from cradle to cradle until it finally fell asleep.*	Rather than cradle-to-grave focus, this more specific spin on sustainability to use the unprocessed, whole end-of-life product as raw material for a new product. *The exasperated operations manager begged the CC2C professors at the conference to come look at what sustainability means in real life.*
Crowd Sourcing kraʊd 'sɔr sɪŋ - verb Address a crowd to ask for money, but not a hold-up nor begging. *"Kind people, please give me your money"*	Extract money from a crowd of small donors. Upside: fairly anonymous way of raising small sums of cash. Downside: donors think they're buying a finished product that will go to market. *John posted a flashy rendering of his product on a crowdsourcing platform to lure people into funding the idea.*
Data Cleaning 'deɪ tə 'kli nɪŋ - verb To remove outliers and obvious errors from data sets. *After noticing the thermometer had broken during the 7th of 10 measurement cycles, the laboratory assistant removed the last four sets*	When collecting large data sets from messy sources (like panels of uninterested, paid respondents) the incoming material often includes high percentages of unusable garbage. *Having sent out 20,000 surveys on fragranced contact lenses, the lack of serious response drove Janet nuts. Cleaning the data got her a theoretically correct diagnostic though.*

Normal People	Innovation People
Data Mining ˈdeɪ tə ˈmaɪ nɪŋ - verb To dig into a data set in search of something valuable. *We're sitting on 2.7 Tb of customer complaint data. Let's mine that for something to improve our customer satisfaction.*	If your data set is large enough, you can find any pattern you want. *After two weeks of mining data for interesting findings, the analyst concluded she should have gone in with a couple of hypotheses to save time and now she deserved a gin tonic.*
Design Thinking dɪˈzaɪn ˈθɪŋ kɪŋ - verb Think like a designer, especially when solving problems. Simple prototypes, aka Minimal Viable Products, are tested to validate solution principles. *The design team spent some time thinking about a good solution for the client's question.*	Design Thinking, aka insight-led ideation, aka user-centric problem solving is a new name for an established, very effective way of working through iterations of solutions and testing simple prototypes to progress to a good & viable idea. It's reinvented once every Marketer's career, and about four times during every Designer's career. *Disillusioned by lack of commercial success, the innovation team switched to design thinking in order to get to same great solution a skilled designer would have created at a quarter of the cost in half the time but without the authority.*
Design to Value dɪˈzaɪn tu ˈvæl yu - noun Rethink product design and composition to deliver better value, to the manufacturer. *We are going to remove the expensive ingredients from this product and make the new shape 3% smaller, and hope no one notices while I'm still in this job.*	A spin on straightforward cost saving, with the liberty to rethink the structure design or recipe. Works well when the resulting design is openly presented to market as the simpler alternative. Works not so well if introduced as a successor to a more premium previous edition. *Inject air bubbles and call it a mousse.*

Normal People	Innovation People
Digital dɪdʒɪt(ə)l - adjective Relating to, using, or storing data or information in the form of digital signals. *Digital TV, crisper image quality than its analogue predecessor.*	Creating a digital version of whatever was analogue, or without data generation capability before. The prize in sight is using this data for further engagement of the customer, the problem ignored is that some product types are impossible to digitize meaningfully in a non-convoluted way (e.g. food, detergents, toasters). *We sell 45 million packs of toilet paper every year. The QR code has been scanned on at least 34 occasions so we are now feverishly analysing the data this digital experience has generated.*
Disruption dɪsˈrʌp ʃən - noun Disturbance *My movie going experience was severely disrupted by loud munching behind me.*	A disturbance of a market, via a radical new product or service solution. Oddly, most FMCG companies seek to disrupt their own categories rather than someone else's, which I have tried and failed to understand. *We are market leader in the pedal-bin category, and our main innovation objective is to disrupt the pedal-bin category.*
Exit strategy ˈɛg zɪt ˈstræt ɪ dʒi - noun A method of departure, planned ahead of the event triggering departure. *The fire brigade insists every building has a proper exit strategy thought through and implemented via signage.*	Founders of companies who have no intent to stay for very long once VC funding or IPO is secured, will design an exit strategy that allows them to depart with some cash as soon as possible. *Stay away from any start-up where the founders have an exit strategy but no revenue model. Better: stay away from any start-up with no revenue model.*
Gamification ˌgeɪ mə fɪˈkeɪ ʃən - noun To turn an activity into a game. *Lizzy trained her dog to fetch the ball, and thus had gamified an otherwise pointless activity.*	A method to turn tedious activities into something enjoyable, which people will then do without needing to be paid. A competitive element usually helps, as well as assigning 'levels' of experience to progress through, and virtual badge to be earned. *"You earned the Elephant Trunk medal for finishing that nose spray in one hay fever season!"*

Normal People	Innovation People
Hacks hæks - noun Breaking into a system to make it operate differently. Often also refers to shortcuts, usually simplifying a chore of some kind. *He hacked his laundry settings to shorten the cycle by half, by adding 2x more detergent.*	A new word for 'short workshop', hinting of a more modern way that doesn't involve too many post-its and more smart people. Previously known as 'pressure cooker'. *"Let's do an idea hack! Yay!"*
HBR Acronym Short for "Harvard Business Review" a magazine published six times a year by Harvard University, Massachusetts. *Sarah read the latest HBR on the train home.*	THE TRUTH. HBR Articles are heralded by corporate innovators & marketers as the absolute zenith of what is right or wrong in the world of innovation. Creative agencies preferred source of buzzwords for new proposals. *Why Co-Creation? Ha! Haven't you read the latest in HBR on incubation?*
Helicopter with autopilot ˈhɛl ɪˌkɒp tər wɪθ ˈɔ toʊˌpaɪ lət – noun A helicopter that can fly itself in some situations *The helicopter flew itself.*	**OMG!! IT'S A FLYING CAR!**
Incubator ɪn kyəˌbeɪ tər – noun A device to nurture fragile young organisms through an early stage of life. *The prematurely born baby thrived after a difficult few weeks in the incubator*	See: '**Accelerator**' *The hair-splitting debate over the differences between an Accelerator and an Incubator left everyone exhausted, annoyed and none the wiser. The chances of success didn't improve either way.*
Insight ˈɪnˌsaɪt – noun A deep understanding, of human behaviour. *"OMG that's SO true" versus "Yeah, true".*	The term 'insight' lost its magical potency around 2012, when it started to be used for any snippet of data, hypothesis, random fact or rumour. *The team browsed the internet for insight into the life of Generation Z.*

Normal People	Innovation People
Internet of Things, IoT ˈɪn tərˌnɛt ʌv θɪŋ - noun Devices connected via the internet *Our alarm system is IoT enabled, the camera, movement detector and taser all have their own IP address and are controlled by this app.* *IoT's valuable application is in devices traditionally connected by cables, or where 'dumb' can be made 'smart' by hooking up to a central server.*	To connect an electrical device to any other electrical device, or app - without too much concern about any need or added value from connecting them - and implemented with cheap, inferior programming skills. Known examples are cat feeders that starve cats, barbecues that don't work outside of wifi-range, and we've had connected fridges since 1997 that still no one has found a purpose for. *Wow, I can now toast my bread to perfectly fit my mood by answering the seven simple questions on my phone's MyToast™ app.*
Lean startup lin ˈstartˌʌp - noun A method of building a business when you don't know if there is a problem to solve, nor what the solution might then be, nor how the money flows. *Lean start-up was heralded as the best innovation approach for large organisations, because that generation of their innovation teams would rather have worked for a startup than a big corporation.*	Just don't, please. *"Because our brand had failed to show any meaningful growth over the past 4 years, they agreed the best way forward was to hire 4 college graduates with no category experience and put them in a separate room with a Ping-Pong table to innovate them out of trouble. Now three and a half years in, we're excited to what will come out!"*
Omni-channel brand ʌmnɪ ˈtʃæn l brænd - noun Covers all channels. *Lego® is an omni-channel brand, with their market manifestations covering product, gaming, social media, movies, television and theme parks,*	Every FMCG brand team wants to break out of their mould, and usually refers to Lego® as the aspiring example. *How do we make our world-leading brand of tinned tuna more omni-channel like Lego®?*

Normal People	Innovation People
Pledge plɛdʒ - noun Formal word for promise, often expressed to an anonymous audience rather than someone who will hold you accountable. *He pledged to never drink one drop of alcohol again, after 2025.*	A nice way for corporate leadership to rally the troops behind an ambitious goal, without too much concern over practicalities of achieving it. Almost without exception the start of a life of pain for middle management. *Snack food CEO's have recently been out-bidding each other for the greenest 2025 pledges.*
Pretotype pri:tətʌɪp - noun A first or preliminary version of a device or product to test solution principles. *The firm is testing a pretotype of the new can opener, to test whether opening it at the bottom really is as good an idea as they hope.*	Also known as Minimal Viable Product (MVP), a simplified design to test for viability. Not to be confused with Prototype (full design made by R&D) or Pilot Run (first trials on final production assets). *As Pretotype, the R&D team gave their test panel cereal cracker, a spoonful of strawberry jam and photo of a smiling woman. The results were disappointing and they dropped their hypothesis.*
Pivot ˈpɪv ət - verb To spin around an axis. *The ballet dancer skilfully and elegantly pivoted from left to right and back.*	To change your mind, and your business plan, because the old idea didn't work or you didn’t think it through properly. As long as there is an idiot willing to pay, there is no limit to the number of pivots you can make. *They couldn’t figure a way to make money from squeezing juice from a pouch but then went bust before they could pivot for the seventh time.*

Normal People	Innovation People
Purpose ˈpɜr pəs - noun Aspirational goal towards one strives, often immaterial and related to character or state of being. *Charlotte's purpose in life was to visit every capital on the planet starting with a 'C'. But without a penny to spend on travel, she quickly parked the idea of visiting Canberra, Caracas, Cairo, Columbo and Cape Town... and instead settled on Cardiff as the capital of Wales for now.*	Retrofitting onto your brand an ethical, aspirational or simply more palatable reason for existence than 'to make money'. The reality of course being that brands who broadcast their (newfound) purpose loudly tend to overlook how genuine purpose drives all brand & organisational actions and not merely their communications. *The brand team campaigned hard across all their social media channels, on how government should be much more ambitious on the sustainability agenda. But journalists quickly spotted they had been fined twice in a year for excess CO2 emissions, and had paid less than 1% in tax for over a decade.*
SaaS Acronym The conversion of any product or single-use service into subscription service via the internet. *The photo editing software team created a cloud version of their graphics packages and now charges a pay-per-month fee instead of offering the program for sale as they had for decades before.*	For software companies, this has been a great way to keep making money well after the upgrades stopped being worth buying the upgrade for. This has alerted manufacturers of physical goods to consider ways of creating services around their products worth paying a subscription for. Works well for business PR, less so for top line revenue. *Having lost the razorblade home delivery wars, the company pivoted to SaaS (Shaving as a Service) and now sends barbers out to their customers bathrooms.*
Sprint sprɪnt - noun Run at full speed over a short distance. *I saw Charlie sprinting through traffic towards me*	Subset or cluster of activities in an Agile process, as part of a series of iterations *We've been in field since sprint #6, and will continue sprinting until the cows come home.*

Normal People	Innovation People
Storytelling ˈstɔr iˌtɛl ɪŋ - verb Human history is recorded through storytelling. *Patrick's rendition of the miracle was hampered by his lack of storytelling skill.*	The magic that ties loose sand into proud shrines of compelling logic. Contrary to fiction writing, or real life, storytelling is explicitly about creating a narrative that holds truths together into a believe whole. *The data analytics team stopped hiring data scientists and instead recruited former movie script writers to create the boardroom reports.*
Strategy ˈstræt ɪ dʒi	Tactics, coherent response to event
Tactics ˈtæk tɪks	Panic, knee-jerk response to event
TED Talk tɛd tɔk – noun TED Conferences (acronym for Technology, Entertainment, Design) is an American media organization that posts 20 minute talks online under the slogan "ideas worth spreading"... *"TED Has some great talks on cartooning and art".*	On par with HBR articles, but easier to browse and process by innovators with short attention spans. Used by creative agencies to spice up workshop materials with intriguing thought pieces, which is remarkable as it makes the TED presenter appear much more interesting & intelligent than the agency representative. *"♡ OMG SIMON SINEK OMG ♡" babbled the CMO in her newsletter*
Transformation ˌtræns fərˈmeɪ ʃən - noun Entering a new state of being. *I met Bob when he was a fit young man, but over time he transformed into Bob The Blob.*	A rethink of the business' future, ideally to make it resilient to change and thrive in a future somewhere 5-10 years out. Or at least beyond the expected tenure of the leadership team, and setting an aspiring ambition for their successors. Successful transformation is one of the few innovative journeys that has to start top-down, but the challenge in practice is proper follow-through on long time scales. *Just look at Disney® over the past 60 years; there's your benchmark*

Normal People	Innovation People
Use Case yus keɪs - noun In software engineering, a use case is a list of actions defining the interactions between a role (actor) and a system to achieve a goal. *She demonstrated how her new finance app worked, with a couple of use cases around counting, lending, laundering and hiding small sums of money.*	A somewhat paradoxical proof point for explaining how amazing your *new* idea is, by showing how it's already been done before by someone else. *The board wasn't convinced the idea was radical enough, nor that it would provide an ROI worth the risk. So they asked the team to provide a few use cases to help them decide*
White space waɪt speɪs - noun Empty space in a document, or squash court. *In the formal departure communication, there was no whitespace left for her to scribble her parting message to the team.*	A market gap, mystical opportunity that no one, neither in the business nor a competitor has spotted before. In practice, an area the brand itself hasn't operated in, nor a direct competitor. But given the density of consumer offers in any FMCG category the likelihood of such a unicorn opportunity to exist is dismal. *As market leader in shaving cream foam, the board agreed that shaving cream gels was a real white space worth conquering.*
Workout session ˈwɜrkˌaʊt ˈsɛʃ ən - noun A period of intense activity. *The Crossfitter® really looked forward to her 5am workout session in the pouring rain.*	A new word for "workshop", hinting to something more active than sitting in a chair all day. *We have six workout sessions scheduled and now working out which ones will be live, and which will be run through Teams.*

If you don't have this one already ...

thoughts from a
GRUMPY
innovator
written & illustrated by costas papaikonomou

Order one now. I hear it's funny.

Premise of the 1st Grumpy Book

Anyone celebrating the tenacity of successful innovators is probably ignoring the far larger number of tenacious idiots pursuing bad ideas. If you think about the classic description of what character traits help people succeed in turning an innovative idea into a profitable business stream – winners and losers at this particular game are frighteningly similar:

- ***Dogged determination***
- ***Blind devotion to their idea***
- ***Unshakable confidence, against all odds***

There must be a fine line between getting it very right or very wrong. In fact, I think there's a paradox hidden in there.

Companies are structured entities, with defined procedures and efficient processes that ensure things get done. Even the messiest of businesses are organized to some level. In stark contrast, the *reality* they operate in is unpredictable, fluid, ugly and most of all: immense. In this simple contrast lies a beautiful paradox: it is the reason there will always be new opportunities & needs for new things *and* it is the main reason for failing at successfully doing so. The attributes that guarantee new opportunities are the opposite of what an efficient corporate system thrives upon.

The chart on the next page shows how the four capabilities crucial to running a business are hampered in the context of innovation[4]. Within the neatly controlled corporate

---

[4] *Yes, you can slice business up many other ways too. But this particular way happens to work well for my story.*

ecosystem, they do as they're asked to and all is fine – as long as they keep looking inward.

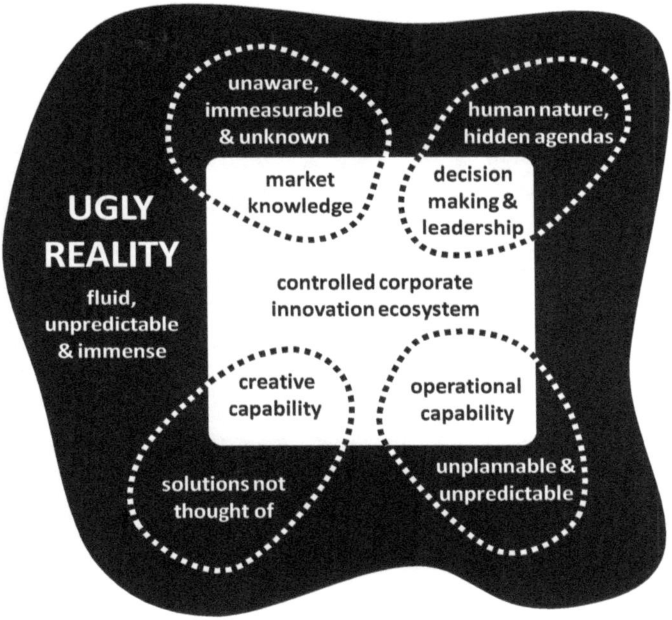

I've found most of the failures in innovation can be brought back to individuals and teams in denial of the reality outside of their campus walls, totally unnecessarily.

This little book holds some of the thoughts I had seeing this happen. If you have experience in the innovation arena, you may recognize attitudes, situations and odd behaviours. Don't worry, we'll keep those our little secret.

Costas Papaikonomou
June 2012

Or this one?

Second
thoughts from a
GRUMPY
innovator

Order that now too. It’s even funnier.

Premise of the 2nd Grumpy Book

In the first Grumpy Innovator book I explored the paradox of innovation[5]. The conflict between a messy, ever-changing outside world which drives the need to innovate, versus wanting a predictable, calm environment in which it is easier to run a profitable business. In corporate ecosystems, this leads to over-relying on models and abstract views of the world, resulting in poor success rates. It was also fun to throw rocks at various functions who we all know get in the way of things more than anything.

What I'd like to explore with you in this second book is a number of perspectives on 'innovation' itself. What is it, how does it strain people & processes and what core competencies does a business need to do it well? But most of all to throw a couple more rocks and have some fun.

On the next two pages is a diagram showing the Sunny Smile of Innovation alongside its dark mirror image, the Murky Mechanics of Innovation. We'll explore how innovation is more than the business textbook definition of 'doing something new that makes money' or 'drives growth'. It comes in different shades and cannot be seen without its implications on the organisation delivering it.

---

[5] *You can find the first book's premise on page 155*

Sunny Smile Of Innovation

Innovation is a commercial tool for businesses to continuously seek out new revenue opportunities, and

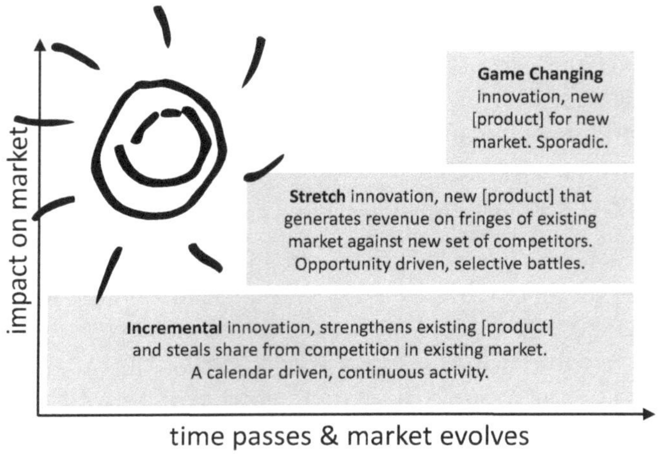

impact on market
Game Changing innovation, new [product] for new market. Sporadic.
Stretch innovation, new [product] that generates revenue on fringes of existing market against new set of competitors. Opportunity driven, selective battles.
Incremental innovation, strengthens existing [product] and steals share from competition in existing market. A calendar driven, continuous activity.
time passes & market evolves

that's the bright happy side shown here.

- **Incremental**: this is your 'new news' process. Small tweaks to satisfy new questions from existing users/clients and piss off competition.
- **Stretch**: find new occasions and formats to draw in an audience just beyond your current reach. Great if you're starting to lose on price in your current market and things are commoditizing.
- **Game Changers**: The sexy end of the spectrum, where you create a lasting legacy, get your face on magazine covers and re-invent the industry.

Murky Mechanics Of Innovation

When most business books and creative gurus talk about 'disruption', they refer to messing up your competitors' heads and shaking up the market.

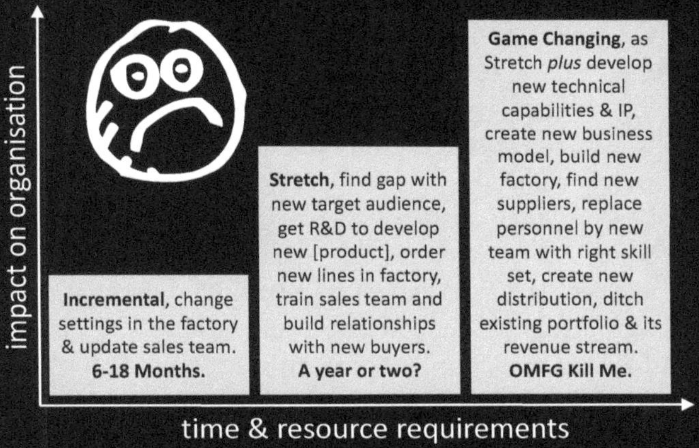

impact on organisation
Incremental, change settings in the factory & update sales team. **6-18 Months.**
Stretch, find gap with new target audience, get R&D to develop new [product], order new lines in factory, train sales team and build relationships with new buyers. **A year or two?**
Game Changing, as Stretch *plus* develop new technical capabilities & IP, create new business model, build new factory, find new suppliers, replace personnel by new team with right skill set, create new distribution, ditch existing portfolio & its revenue stream. **OMFG Kill Me.**
time & resource requirements

That's *not* it. You are disrupting yourself much more.

- **Incremental**: a cross-functional effort you can tightly plan and control, within set ecosystems.
- **Stretch**: Requires understanding new category consumers and business rules, creation of minor new capability and your best bet for growing your market when you're still calling the shots.
- **Game Changers**: Only when your back is against the wall, your current [product] is completely commoditized or the market is going extinct.

So what does this dark and disheartening mirror image mean? It shows that not only do you need particular functions inside your business to innovate pragmatically in a messy world to keep the machines running[6], you also need an additional set of meta-capabilities to adapt your organisation as much as the market you're serving;

- The ability to share responsibility for innovation across functions; in parallel, not sequentially, with the lead switching sensibly as the work progresses. Similarly, realising that the source of the opportunity can come from anywhere too – sales, technology, distribution, etcetera – *not* just consumer focus groups and market research.
- Acute awareness of the required impact your innovation needs to make in order to achieve your business objective. Create an incremental innovation when that'll do the job, reserve game changers for when you need (or can afford) one.
- Savvy use of expensive assets over time, retaining function and relevance beyond the initially intended launch products and support future revenue as well.
- Install processes across the business functions that drive for value-add to the end result, your product. Not solely to optimize operational efficiency. It is the simplest way to ensure you keep aiming for relevancy *and* pick up early signals of change right at the source: the customers of your products and services.
- Acknowledgment that when you move up into Stretch and Game Changing innovation, you are also moving *away* from daily procedures and into new ball games with unknown rules. That means success will depend more than anything on the judgment of the people

---

[6] *See first Grumpy Innovator book*

creating the innovation, not on prescribed ways of working. *Trust* them.

I'll share my grumpy thoughts on pitfalls on these five principles, along with ways that might make life just a little easier. Might. A little.

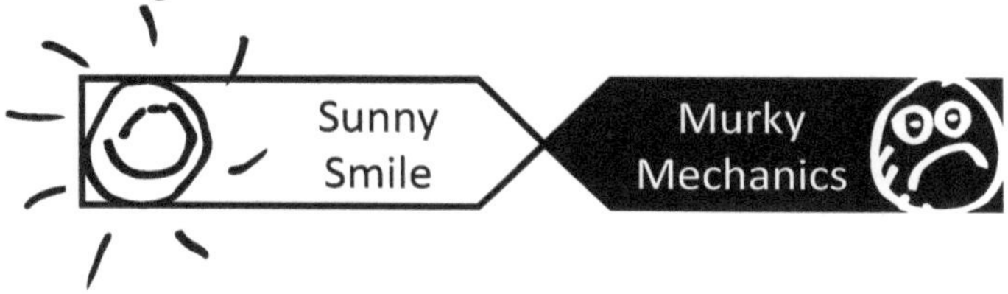

You may now be thinking... wait a moment, aren't today's celebrated new heroes of innovation in the digital arena doing all that Game Changing in the blink of an eye *and* making a fortune on the go?

Yes – *and*.

Putting those new digital heroes in a more realistic and perhaps even cynical perspective;

- The vast majority of the global economy runs on businesses who *make* things, not on digital platforms for selling or accessing them. This will remain the case in our lifetime, at least as long as humans consume physical foods & goods.
- Most, if not *all* billion-dollar start-ups prove to be pyramid schemes, not making any profitable revenue stream, ever. Then they collapse.
- The digital space is big and sexy, but it's also an immature Wild West in comparison to say, laundry detergents, chewing gum or dry soups.

This book is for people who are in the business of making and selling real things, to highly competitive mass markets around the globe. People building brands by carefully crafting relevant improvements to win their consumers' hearts. For them, the Murky Mechanics Of Innovation are a reality that tires them by day and keeps them awake at night.

I salute you.

Costas Papaikonomou
June 2015

Further salutations

A big THANK YOU to my fellow founders and our incredible teams at Happen & Winkle. You are the reason I get out of bed in the morning. Albeit only if I'm not out of bed already for being with my wife and children first.

Another big THANK YOU to all the client teams who not only challenge us daily with delightful innovation questions, but also laugh with us about the peculiarities this work often brings.

And THANK YOU anonymous reader of this book.
I hope it made you smile, it was a pleasure writing. Get in touch to let me know your thoughts, your messages are very welcome.

Thank you all,

Costas Papaikonomou

Twitter: @grumpyinnovator
Email: costas@grumpyinnovator.com

Printed in Poland
by Amazon Fulfillment
Poland Sp. z o.o., Wrocław

30976027R00091